SAFE IN THE STREETS:
DON'T BE A VICTIM

SAFE IN THE STREETS: DON'T BE A VICTIM

Sandra J. Merwin

FORMERLY TITLED: *NOT A VICTIM*

THE
BOOK
PEDDLERS
OF DEEPHAVEN

©Copyright 1982, 1985 Sandra J. Merwin

All rights reserved. No part of this publication may be reproduced, stored in a retrieval system or transmitted in any form or by any means, electronic, mechanical, photocopying, recording, or otherwise without the prior written permission of the author.

Library of Congress Catalog Card Number:

ISBN: 0-916773-03-5
ISBN: 0-916773-04-3 (hdc.)
(Formerly ISBN: 0-9610642-0-X; EM PRESS)

10 9 8 7 6 5 4 3 2 1

Printed in the United States of America

For information address

All Rights Reserved...

All the characters mentioned in this book are fictional and any resemblance to any living person is purely coincidental.

To the victims' — may it never happen again.

Contents

Chapter	Page
Acknowledgements	8
Introduction	9
Foreward	11
1 Prevention Defense	13
2 Roadblocks	15
3 Attitude for Survival	21
4 NonVerbals: Body Language Tells	25
5 Safety: A Habit	36
6 Decisions: What to Do and When to Do It	49
7 Survival Alternatives	54
8 Just for Women	74
9 Please, Help the Children	87
10 Should I Fight?	94
11 The Experts Talk	100
Epilogue	105
Recommended Readings	106

Acknowledgements

I want to express my sincere appreciation to Pat Worley, John Worley, Larry Carnahan, Gordon Franks, and the instructors of Mid-American Karate, who taught me valuable information about myself and my abilities to survive.

Introduction

I began this book because I saw a need for it. I wanted to feel safe. Others told me they had the same concerns. I began looking for information that I called "preventive defense." I found books on what to do after you were raped or victimized. I found information on how to defend yourself if an attacker was approaching, but I found very little information that advised me what to do to prevent becoming a victim. As very few people stop at the library on the way home from being victimized, I decided to write a "before book," a book that explains what to do, now, to keep yourself safe.

Foreword

Have you chosen not to be a victim? Everyday people make hundreds of choices: What color to wear? What to have for lunch? Whether to have that extra dessert? What television programs to watch? How to spend your money?, etc. Along with these choices, each individual has the choice not to be a victim. Every man, woman, and child, has the choice not to be a victim. To choose not to be a victim means you must take some action and do some thinking, now!

This book is designed to help you make the choice not to be a victim today. The first chapters focus on preventive actions. Special areas of concern for women and children and basic self defense alternatives are discussed in later chapters.

This book was written with two basic objectives in mind.

They are as follows:

I. The reader can expect to develop a more healthy awareness of prevention defense.

II. The reader will have the opportunity to consider now, the choices and options available if and when a dangerous situation occurs.

1
Prevention Defense

Prevention defense begins now, not with the attack of an aggressor. Prevention defense starts with your state of mind. First, it is necessary to accept that individuals have the right and responsibility to keep themselves safe and free from harm. This responsibility includes prevention defense. Prevention is defined: "to take action ahead of; to keep from happening; to hinder or to stop." In this context, defense is defined as the ability to resist attack. Prevention defense refers to "taking action before" that will hinder, stop or develop the ability to resist or circumvent an attack.

The elements involved in developing prevention defense are: attitude, action, and awareness. Attitude refers to the mental determination and commitment necessary to develop habits of safety and defense. Actions refer to preventive actions and defense responses. Awareness means the mental alertness and understanding of; your physical environment, your abilities to protect yourself, and your abilities to prevent potentially dangerous situations.

Anyone can start developing habits of prevention defense. Approximately 80 percent of what we do, we do without conscious thought. for example; people first learning to drive a car, think about steering, maneuvering, and shifting. Veteran drivers drive without conscious thought of driving procedures. They converse, smoke, listen to music or think of other topics while they drive to and from work.

When people first learn to drive, they must concentrate on learning safe procedures. The same is true of prevention defense. When first learning prevention defense, individuals must take care to develop these new safe behaviors. After a period of time, the prevention defense skills will become habits. Developing prevention defense habits will take several months of conscious focus on attitude, awareness and alternative actions.

2
Roadblocks

Many people set up roadblocks. These roadblocks are thoughts and beliefs that may effect a person's ability to remain safe. To develop a healthy attitude about prevention defense, let's address the major roadblocks.

ROADBLOCK #1 "It won't happen to me."

Erroneous Thinking

The assault statistics are just numbers. Numbers aren't flesh and blood people. I'm a person, not a number, therefore I am safe.

Reality

Each assault statistic represents only those reported assaults. Many assaults and rapes are not reported. Each number represents a human being who has feelings of outrage, fear, repulsion, and indignation, just to name a few.

Productive Thinking

It can happen to me. I won't live in terror or paralyzing fear, waiting for something to happen. Instead, I will take actions that will increase my safety and peace of mind.

ROADBLOCK #2 "Someone will protect me."

Erroneous Thinking

Frequently people declare:

"The police will protect me."

"My husband will take care of my safety."

"As long as I'm in a public area someone will come to my aid."

This type of thinking adds up to the belief; "I'm not responsible for my own safety." We abdicate our responsibility and expect others to shoulder the burden.

Reality

The police are committed to serving and protecting individuals, but they may be overworked in your area. If a police officer is available, by all means allow the officer to take charge. But, can you always guarantee you'll have an officer near you? The same thing is true of a husband or a crowd of people. Can you guarantee someone will always be available to protect you?

Productive Thinking

As I cannot always depend on another to keep me safe, I must take responsible actions for my own safety.

ROADBLOCK #3 "I could never win over a larger stronger attacker so why try."

Erroneous Thinking

This roadblock can be best summarized:

"Bigger, larger, taller, stronger people have all the advantages, I might as well be up against a 'super person.'"

Reality

No matter what size, the aggressor can still feel pain in vulnerable areas. You do not have to win! If an aggressor attacks you, you are not in a tournament where someone wins and someone loses. You do have other alternatives.

Productive Thinking

Even if a large person is the aggressor, I do have choices. I will carefully consider my choices of prevention and defense.

ROADBLOCK #4 "I couldn't hurt anybody."

Erroneous Thinking

Many people believe that they could never physically hurt another human being.

Reality

Only rare individuals want to inflict hurt and pain on others. It may be your fear of getting hurt that stops you from defending or protecting yourself. Everyone has the right to use the necessary physical force to stop an attacker.

Productive Thinking

I have the right to protect and defend my body. No one has the right to hurt or victimize me.

ROADBLOCK #5 "I don't want to think about it, it frightens me."

Erroneous Thinking

"I deny that anything can happen to me."

"It is just too unpleasant to think about."

"I feel frightened and afraid when I think about an aggressor attacking me."

"I don't like being afraid so I'll ignore it."

Many people choose to ignore the whole idea that anything could happen to them because it is just too painful to consider.

Reality

Ignoring a situation won't make it go away. Few people enjoy thinking about frightening, threatening situations. Facing an unpleasant situation and developing preventive actions, gives an individual a sense of self worth and autonomy.

Productive Thinking

Even though I have fearful feelings, I will think through my prevention and defense alternatives.

ROADBLOCK #6 "If I fight an attacker, I'll make it worse."

Erroneous Thinking

"If I defend myself from an attacker, I might make him mad, and I'll make the situation worse."

Reality

Some attackers do not expect victims to try to defend themselves. Often aggressors feel there is a hidden script that the victim should follow; the victim should plead, shake and cry. Assertive behavior and self defense may surprise your attacker and scare him away. The insistent attacker may become angry if you hurt him a little. If you choose defense, your defense must be committed to strong techniques that will startle and scare the attacker.

Productive Thinking

I will use all my preventive techniques to avert attack, however, if I am attacked, I may choose strong and determined actions.

ROADBLOCK #7 "I'm too shy...old...fat...young...uncoordinated... feminine...to protect myself."

Erroneous Thinking

This belief is summed up best:

Because I'm too_____(fill in the blank), there's nothing I can do to protect and defend myself.

Reality

Almost everyone seems to have some personal belief about their physical or mental abilities to defend themselves, but everyone can take preventive actions to insure personal safety.

Productive Thinking

Even though I am_____(fill in blank), I will take action to protect and defend my personal safety.

ROADBLOCK #8 "I don't want to become paranoid about my safety, I want to enjoy life."

Erroneous Thinking

"If I think about all the awful things that can happen to me, I'll spend all my time looking for bogeymen at each corner. If I really think about it, I'll become so concerned about my safety, that I won't leave my house."

Reality

Identifying and understanding a problem can help people deal more effectively with the situation. By identifying and developing an awareness of potentially dangerous situations, we then can plan alternatives. This reality doesn't need to frighten people only make them more aware. Awareness helps people become more cautious and careful about personal safety. You will not feel that false sense of security, but you can feel comfortable and aware that you've taken steps to be prepared.

Productive Thinking

I may not feel that warm feeling of false security, but I will have a feeling of being in charge of my personal safety through my preventive actions.

ROADBLOCK #9 "You have to have years and years of training before you can do anything to protect yourself."

Erroneous Thinking

A common belief is that it takes years of physical training to do anything to protect yourself.

Reality

There are many actions you can take to protect yourself that do not involve physical training. Even a short self defense course can help you become more aware and better able to protect yourself.

Productive Thinking

I can and will take actions that will increase my ability to protect and defend myself.

ROADBLOCK #10 "I live in a safe environment."

Erroneous Thinking

People often give these excuses for not becoming involved in insuring their own safety.

"We have a nice quiet neighborhood, there's no need for me to worry."

"There haven't been any assaults in our town. The assaults happen someplace else."

"I know everyone in our area, no one would do any harm to me."

Reality

People are mobile. Even if your city, neighborhood or suburb is fenced, patrolled and padlocked, you cannot guarantee that all members of your community are **not** aggressors. Perhaps your area has a low crime rate. Will your low crime rate continue as your neighborhood grows older and changes? In a large number of rapes or assaults, the victim and aggressor know each other. Just because you recognize an individual doesn't mean he's harmless.

Productive Thinking

I will not be lulled into a false sense of security by my environment.

I will plan and take actions to increase my safety in each environment I encounter.

Please take a few minutes and consider the following question:

What roadblocks have prevented you from taking responsibility for your personal safety?

3
Attitude for Survival

Your attitude is one of the most important aspects of prevention defense. The first step in developing a "prevention defense attitude," is to make a commitment to yourself. The commitment is to take responsibility for your well being.

I made my commitment when I was 21.

My husband was in the Navy. We were newly married when we moved from a small Montana town where I grew up, to the deep South. Because base housing was overflowing, we were quartered in a mobile home park. Block after block all you could see were mobile homes that housed Navy personnel. On either side of the mobile home park were empty lots with trees and brush. Our trailerhouse was located next to one of these empty lots. The day my husband left for indoctrination battalion, three blocks of Marines picked up their families and sailed to their duty stations in the Mediterranean. Suddenly I was totally isolated and alone. My husband could not get in touch with me for three weeks, and my entire neighborhood was empty. After living this way for several days, I prepared to go to bed one evening and had an uneasy feeling I was being watched. I discounted this feeling as a case of nerves and crawled into bed. I must have dozed for awhile. I awakened with a start. I could see the back door as I lay in bed. I looked toward the door and saw the knob move. My heart pounded loudly in my ears. I was paralyzed with fear. After what seemed like an eternity, I crawled out of bed, down the hall and to the telephone in the kitchen. In the dark I lifted the telephone off the receiver and dialed "0".

"This is the operator," a female voice said. I stated my name and address, and said: "Someone is trying to break into my house." She responded with, "Just a minute please, I'll connect you with the police." After several minutes a man's voice said, "Hello, this is Sergeant Adams."

I again said my name, address, and explained that someone was trying to break in. After several seconds he responded, "I'm sorry, your address is on the division between city and county. You are not in our jurisdiction. Please wait. I'll look up the Sheriff's number."

As I waited by the phone, I saw the front door knob begin to move. When the policeman gave me the Sheriff's number, I was so shaken I couldn't remember it. I asked him to repeat it so I could write it down. I turned on a light to see what I was writing. When the light flooded the room I heard someone leap off the front steps and run. The sound of footsteps seemed to halt at the garage. I wrote down the number and immediately called the Sheriff. Once again I repeated my name and address, and explained that someone was trying to break in. The Sheriff had his radio tuned to one of the country western stations. He said, "I can't hear you. Let me turn down the music." I waited in terror as the volume was turned down. Then I heard a voice ask, "Now what is it?" I again repeated my name and address and explained that someone was trying to break in. The Sheriff replied he would send someone right out to check the situation.

I moved to the window in the living room and huddled behind the couch. Sandwiched between the curtains and the window, I watched the road and the garage. I held my breath as I saw the outline of a man blend into the deep shadows next to the garage. I waited three and a half hours. The Sheriff never showed up. I don't know when the man near the garage slipped off into the night. When the sun began to rise, I was still sandwiched between the window and the curtains, watching the road, waiting for my protection to come.

Later that morning I called the liaison officer. He was the person who was supposed to relay information to my husband if I had a problem. I told the liaison officer someone had tried to break in, and I was terrified he would return. I also explained no one came to help. The liaison officer replied in crisp military tones, "There is nothing I can do to help you. It's your problem!" He advised me not to tell my husband as my spouse had enough to do without worrying about a frightened wife.

That was the beginning of a month long ordeal. Each night as I prepared to go to bed, I thought about the intruder and wondered if he would return. Then I listened to each noise and each movement, expecting the person to return. After three weeks of sleepless nights and terror, I was awakened by a noise coming from the roof. In my mind the whole situation was happening all over again. I was threatened. I was in mortal danger and no one would come to help. Suddenly I was angry. I was so angry that rage filled every pore of my body. Without thinking I leaped out of bed, walked into the kitchen, took out a knife and charged into the street wearing only my nightgown and pink bathrobe. The knife glistened in the street light as I screamed, "Who's there?" At that moment a cat yowled, jumped from a garbage can and disappeared into the night.

As I look back at the situation, I realize it was not very sensible to go storming out into the night wearing a pink bathrobe, and wielding a knife. I did learn from the situation. I learned that your attitude and determination are the two things you need most in any self defense situation. Most of all I learned I had to take responsibility for myself. I couldn't always have a husband to protect me. I couldn't always depend on my neighbors. I learned a very valuable lesson; I had to take responsibility for myself, responsibility not to be a victim, responsibility to be able and capable of defending and protecting myself.

I had to face an unpleasant situation. Everyone has to face unpleasant situations in life. Our attitude may determine whether we survive the situation. How people react to a situation can be summarized in the example of two people climbing a mountain. The mountain is steep and rocky. Both fall. But one person lies there and cries: "Why is this mountain so steep? The world shouldn't be this way! It's not fair!" This is the person who places his responsibility for what's happening on others. The other person stands up, dusts himself off and says, "I've got to learn to climb more carefully. I'm climbing this mountain because I choose to climb this mountain. I'm going to have to learn to keep myself safe." Both people have problems. One person refuses to be stopped by those problems. That person chooses actions to take responsibility for himself.

In order to take responsibility for yourself, you have to take three steps. The first step is to identify those areas or actions that place you in a victim status. Identify all the beliefs and behaviors that keep you from taking responsibility for yourself. The second step is to take responsibility for your own behavior and safety. The third step is to have an action plan for threatening situations. An action plan involves thinking through and considering your choices and options so that in any situation, at a moment's thought, you know your choices and alternative options.

There is only one attitude that will make your action plan work for you. You must believe with all your heart that you have responsibility for your own life, and you have choices of how to act and react.

4
NonVerbals: Body Language Tells

Many people have heard the cliche': "Actions speak louder than words." Communications experts phrase the idea, "Seventy to eighty percent of your communications are nonverbal." Experts in martial arts say; "Your confidence shows in your body carriage." Many books and articles have been written on the importance of body language.

Betty Grayson and Morris I. Stein, address the nonverbal behavior of victims in their article, "Attracting Assault: Victims' Nonverbal Cues", in the winter, 1981, **Journal of Communication.**[1]

Although their study is not conclusive evidence, it does suggest that victims may have nonverbal movements in common. In the study, convicted prisoners were asked to view videotapes of sixty pedestrians and rate their "assault potential." The assault ratings varied from "Easy rip off", to "Would avoid it, too big a situation." Then the researchers had experts in movement variables analyze the nonverbal movements of the pedestrians. Some common movements characterized the potential victims just as several common motions characterized the nonvictims. This study is evidence which suggests victims may signal or clue aggressors that they are easy targets.

It's as if the aggressor needs a victim to fulfill a specific role or to act a script, and the aggressor carefully chooses a victim to play the part. Joel Kirsch, a clinical psychologist from California, suggests that an aggressor is dependent upon his victim, to "actually take on the role of victim." The aggressor must "attract and hold the attention of his victim long enough to create a context conducive to attacking the person."[2] In order to create the context Kirsch refers to, the aggressor may use fear, surprise or force to his advantage. The aggressor must somehow unbalance his victim so that he can create a situation of attack.

Surprise, fear and force are used as weapons to unbalance the potential victim. As soon as the victim loses his balance the aggressor has the power to choose the script. The word balance is used to describe both a physical and an emotional state of being. Balance refers to physical equilibrium and harmonious state of mind. When people stumble, their physical balance deteriorates. When people are angry or fearful, their emotional balance may turn to discord. Just as it is easy to push a person down if he is already stumbling, so it is easy to victimize the person who is caught off balance emotionally and physically.

Developing personal balance may be your most important prevention defense. A person who possesses a mental and physical harmony, sends a nonverbal message to his attacker. The message says, "I am balanced. I am in charge of my mental and physical being. I will not be easy to unbalance. Therefore, I will not easily submit to a role in your script."

To develop personal balance, you must first increase your physical and mental awareness. The following exercise is designed to help you experience the balanced state.

DEVELOPING PHYSICAL AWARENESS

First stand with your feet a shoulder's distance apart. Your stance is extremely important. How you stand is your physical balance. Balance your weight between the soles and balls of your feet. To do this, move your weight forward to the balls of your feet, then shift your weight back to your heels. Continue doing this slowly until you find your natural balance between the soles and the balls of your feet. Be sure your knees are neither locked nor deeply bent. You should feel comfortable and relaxed. Make sure your heels are not on the same line. The heels should be slightly separate for maximum stability.

As you stand in this position, take a deep breath. Let your lungs fill and your belly expand outward. Touch yourself about an inch and a half to two inches below your naval. This is your gravitational center of balance. Focus your thinking on your center of balance as you continue to take deep relaxing breaths. Move your head slowly forward and back until you feel your head balance effortlessly on your neck. As you continue to stand in your balanced stance, allow your mind to relax. Relax your facial muscles and your eyes. To relax your eyes, do not look at any specific object, merely allow your eyes to relax by going out of focus. This is a balanced state. Your nonverbal behavior reveals neither a victim nor an aggressor.

To move in a balanced motion is the next step. Continue focusing on your gravitational center as you walk around the room. To maintain your balance as you walk may take practice. To react to an aggressor with balanced nonverbals takes training.

The training begins with an increased awareness of nonverbal and verbal behavior. Your signals are an important factor in prevention defense. Become aware of the signals you may send to an aggressor. Have a friend observe your walking and standing nonverbals and report what they observe.

> Figure 1 helps develop an awareness of your signals. Picture yourself in the situation described in Figure 1 and list your reactions.

Imagine you are walking to your car after work and a stranger approaches you. Picture yourself in this situation and identify your signals.

Signals	Identify your reaction
1. **Eye contact.** What do you look at? Do you look at the stranger? Do you avert eye contact?	
2. **Body posture.** Do you try to make yourself invisible? Do you slump or stand tall?	
3. **Gestures.** Do you use any gestures? Do you keep your hands and arms tightly at your side?	
4. **Voice and tone.** When you speak, how does your voice sound?	
5. **Timing.** Do you hesitate and look uncertain, or do you respond quickly?	
6. **Content.** When you speak, what do you say? Do you apologize? Do you ask questions? Do you give away information about yourself?	
7. **Stride movement.** What is the length of your step? Do you take small mincing steps? Do you take extra long steps? How do your shoes effect your steps?	

8. **Foot movement.** Do you lift and place your foot like you are climbing stairs? Do you walk carefully as if you are walking on eggs? Do you put your heel or the ball of your foot down first? _____

9. **Torso movement.** Do your shoulders and arms move with your hips and legs or at the opposite time? _____

It is important to become aware of the signals or clues you send.

To determine whether your reactions are victim or nonvictim signals, turn to figure 2.

In figure 2, behavior responses are divided into "Victim Behavior" and "Assertive Behavior". Identify any victim signals you listed in figure 1. Then plan time to practice the assertive behavior. Plan to take a walk or go to a shopping center with the purpose of practicing new assertive behaviors so that you begin to feel comfortable with the new signals. Be sure to continue your awareness of the nonverbal signals you send.

FIGURE 1

COMPARING VICTIM AND ASSERTIVE BEHAVIORS

	VICTIM BEHAVIOR	ASSERTIVE BEHAVIOR
Eye Contact:	Head down, eyes down	Look directly at aggressor. Alert, watchful
Body Posture:	Shoulders slumped, arm's held tight "Compacting the body"	Erect, weight evenly distributed
Gestures:	Hands at sides, held tight	Stop or halt gesture, defensive fighting position
Facial Expression:	Blank, frightened, closed, timid	Direct, determined, concentrated
Voice, Tone, etc.:	Squeeky, whispered, pleading, whining	Well modulated, level, direct
Timing:	Hesitation, uncertainty	Quick, spontaneous, reactive, purposeful
Content:	I'm sorry, (apologetic)	"Stop bothering me," (Direct) "Leave me alone" "Take your hands off me."
Stride Movement:	Exaggerated; too short or too long	Medium stride, natural, weight centered
Foot Movement:	Lift and place foot	Heel-to-toe movement
Torso Movement:	Cross movement, right shoulder moving with left hip	Right arm moves with left leg, then left arm moves with right leg
Totality of Movement:	Legs and arms appear to move separately from the body, only parts of the body move	Arms, legs and body move as one

FIGURE 2

NOTES:

Victim behaviors I have identified.

The new assertive behaviors I plan to practice.

ROLE PLAY

To develop more understanding of nonverbal signals, practice role playing. Below are three role-play situations. First, identify and list victim behaviors and assertive behaviors in each situation. Then with a partner act out each part. Take time to experience both the victim behavior and the assertive behavior. This practice allows you to feel the difference between the two behaviors so you can more readily identify when you send victim signals.

Situation	Victim Behavior	Assertive Behavior
A man stands too close to you on an elevator.		
Someone approaches you in a parking lot as you walk to your car. He asks you for a light.		

NONVERBALS: BODY LANGUAGE TELLS

A knock on your door reveals a repairman. He asks to come in.

_____
_____
_____

You're at the water fountain when a man you work with touches you suggestively.

_____
_____
_____

Over 50 percent of our behavior is habitual. We all have habits. Deeply entrenched habits would include: how we walk, eye contact, posture, etc. These nonverbal habits may be difficult to change. If you have discovered some nonverbal signals you want to change, be prepared to spend a month or longer involved in assessing, practicing and thinking about your new nonverbal behaviors. Plan to practice your new behaviors as often as you can for at least a month. Many people experience an uncomfortable feeling when they attempt to use new behaviors. The feeling starts to subside with more practice. Keeping track of your attempts to use new behaviors can assist in determining improvement and persistence. On page 34 is a chart which can be used to keep track of your new nonvictim behaviors.

KEEPING ON TRACK

The goal is to develop nonvictim signals. To reach a goal, it must be attainable and measureable. With practice almost everyone has the ability to develop nonvictim signals. The practice is measureable. Measure your improvement by tracking your attempts to use nonvictim behaviors.

Choose nonverbal responses from figure 2 and report on your success with assertive behaviors.

Day	Situation	New Behavior Used	How it Felt	Results
1				
2				
3				
4				
5				
6				
7				
8				
9				
10				
11				
12				
13				
14				
15				

16 _____
17 _____
18 _____
19 _____
20 _____
21 _____
22 _____
23 _____
24 _____
25 _____
26 _____
27 _____
28 _____
29 _____
30 _____
31 _____

As future studies are done, we may find that assertive nonverbal behavior may be a primary method of prevention defense. Many people involved in martial art's training, develop assertive nonverbals as a by-product of the physical training. For this reason alone, martial art's training may be something to consider in a plan to develop assertive nonverbals.

5
Safety: A Habit

Make your safety a habit. Whether at home, shopping, or traveling, plan for a safe environment. To insure your safety, check your doors, windows, home exterior, and your traveling habits.

DOORS

Locked doors. Develop the habit of keeping your doors locked at all times. Be sure to lock doors: 1) when in your home, 2) when away from home, 3) when traveling in and out of your home such as unloading groceries or working around the yard.

Solid doors. Develop the habit of purchasing security conscious home building materials. For security and energy purposes, solid or ribbed steel doors are better than hollow core doors. Doors with glass may be a security hazard. Break resistant glazing can increase your safety.

Visual door safety. Develop the habit of looking before you open your door. Make sure you have a clear view of the area outside your door. If there is no window from which to view your door, install a peephole with a wide angle lens.

Door structure. Develop the habit of checking your environment for safety. 1) Check your door hinge pins. If the hinge pins are exposed to the outside, jimmy proof your door by pounding a nail in place of a screw from the hinge plate. Let the nail protrude. then drill a hole in the opposite hinge plate so the protruding nail will go into the drilled hole and the door will close. 2) Check for gaps between your door and door frame. Even a small gap can help someone break in.

Door locks. Develop the habit of purchasing the necessary equipment to keep your home secure. 1) A latch bolt is fine, but make sure you also have a deadbolt lock with heavy duty strikers. 2) French doors or swinging doors need one door fitted with verticle throw bolts in addition to the deadbolt and self locking latch on the other door. 3) Make sure locks have a hardened steel collar to protect from tampering. 4) Do not leave keys hidden under your mat, in your flower pot, or any other place around the outside of your home. If you've thought of those spots so has someone else!

Sliding doors. Check the space between the top of the door and the frame. Someone can lift out the door if there's enough space. Put screws into the upper track, leaving just enough room for the door to slide. Use a board, or metal rod in the lower inside rack for further protection.

WINDOWS

Basement windows. If they are not used, secure them permanently with nails or screws.

Windows. Secure windows in at least two areas. Use key locks, wooden dowels, metal rods, nails or pins, to prevent windows from opening all the way.

EXTERIOR

Visual sight line. Trim shrubs away from basement windows. Trim trees and shrubs if they can hide someone at a point of entry.

Lighting outside. Exterior lighting should clearly illuminate entry doors. Flood lights may be helpful in driveways and parking areas.

Lighting inside. 1) Leave a light on all night in your bathroom or kitchen, indicating someone is awake. 2) Use a timer for your lights if you are away at night so they come on automatically. 3) Keep blinds, curtains, and shades closed at night. 4) Open blinds, curtains and shades during the day to show someone is home.

Home maintenance. 1) Do not leave bicycles, lawn mowers, or snowmobiles scattered about outside. (Unattended, unlocked items invite problems.) 2) Keep your house exterior and landscape tidy: i.e. leaves raked, lawn mowed, etc. This indicates the owner is careful and takes precautions. 3) Always keep garage doors closed and locked.

APARTMENT SAFETY

Lighting outside. Notify authorities if lights in lobby or hallway are too dim or out.

Security buildings. Make a habit of keeping your security system secure. Do not leave the door open for anyone else. If a visitor rings the buzzer, his/her friend should let him/her inside. A person with a key in his or her hand doesn't necessarily live in your building. Have a tenants' meeting to discuss how to keep your security. Develop buddy systems for doing laundry.

ELEVATORS

If your apartment building has an elevator, before you get in, make sure it's not going to the roof or basement. Don't get on an elevator with a stranger. Stand near the control panel. If someone gets on the elevator, watch carefully; if you feel uncomfortable, **get off!**

GENERAL

Dogs. Dogs can be excellent protection. Keep your dog near if you think there is danger and allow him access to all of your rooms.

Names. Identify yourself with your last name and initial. Don't use Miss, Mrs. or first names.

Telephone. 1) Never give any personal information over a telephone to a stranger. 2) If you receive a "wrong number" caller, do not give him your correct number. Ask what number he dialed, then tell him to dial again. 3) Hang up immediately on lewd or suspicious phone calls. Then report them to the telephone company or police. 4) Never allow a stranger to know when you'll be gone or if you're home alone. 5) If a stranger requests to talk to another member of your family, do not tell him you're alone. Tell the caller the family member is unavailable and will call him back. 6) If you have babysitters, instruct them to tell your callers you are unavailable and will call back. Instruct them **not** to tell anyone that they are babysitting alone. 7) Children should never tell a caller they are alone. Prepare them with excuses they can use such as, "Dad's in the shower and Mom's taking a nap."

AWAY FROM HOME CHECKLIST

In your car, practice developing the following habits of safety.

1) Always lock your car when leaving it unattended. Lock your car in parking lots, and even in your own driveway.
2) As you unlock your car to get in, look in the back to see if anyone is hiding.
3) As soon as your car is unlocked, get in and lock the door again.
4) Keep your car in good running condition so there will be less chance of getting stranded.
5) Never hide a key anywhere in your car. If you've thought of a place to hide your key, more than likely someone else has also.
6) Park in lighted areas. Avoid parking in unlighted areas.
7) Keep your car's gas tank full so there's less chance of being stranded.
8) Keep car windows closed or only open an inch or two for ventilation.
9) Keep any valuables on the floor of the car, not beside you on the seat.
10) Keep strangers out of your car. If someone follows you or indicates something is wrong, drive to a Police Station or a well lighted, busy service station.

IN PARKING LOTS OR ON THE STREET

Parking lots.

1) Develop the habit of staying alert and watching.
2) Have your keys in your hand and be ready to open your car door **before** you leave the building.
3) Don't walk too close to parked cars where someone maybe hiding in waiting.

4) Know where your car is. Make a strong mental note or write it down.

5) Carry your purse close to your body or under your coat, or not at all.

6) Use a grocery cart or tote bag so your hands can be free to open your car.

7) Be watchful of any alleys, doorways or corners.

On the street.

1) If you are walking, know your route. Know what businesses will be open and where telephones are located. Plan where you will go if you needed help.

2) Dress sensibly.

3) If you use public transit, wait with your back to a wall. Stay in a lighted area. Look alert.

4) Stay away from shrubs, doorways and other hiding areas.

5) Try to walk with companions, or walk near a group of mixed people, both men and women.

TRAVELING

When checking into a motel or hotel, make sure your security is a habit.

1) If the room clerk says your room number out loud, ask for another room assignment. Anyone in the lobby may have heard your room number.

2) Ask for help with your luggage, then fully check your room safety before the bellman leaves.

3) Ask for a room near the front desk or lobby. This means people would be close to respond with help if you need it.

4) Make sure no one else is in the hall near you when you open your door. If someone appears suspicious in the hall, walk immediately to the lobby and request an escort.

5) Put your first initial, last name and your office address on your luggage, so that others will not know your unoccupied home address.

6) Consider purchasing your own portable lock for motel or hotel doors.
7) Don't carry large amounts of money with you. Use credit cards or travelers checks.
8) Be wary of elevators. Get off immediately when you feel uneasy. Don't get on an elevator with one or two lone men.
9) Check out the hotel restaurant before eating there. If the bar is directly connected to the dining area, you may want to eat in your room.
10) Do not give directions to fellow guests. Tell them to ask the front desk.
11) If a stranger appears at your hotel door, do not let him in. If he claims to be a workman call the front desk and verify it.
12) In airports, keep your tickets and money out of sight.
13) Do not load yourself down. Keep your hands free. Check your baggage. Rent a baggage cart or call a porter.
14) If you're going to a city you're not familiar with, get a map. Know exactly how you're going to get to and from your appointments.

Safety Summary Questions

Safety habits are crucial in prevention defense. A brief question and answer format and several "safety situations" will test your knowledge of safety habits.

I. When do you need to be alert?

_____

_____

_____

_____

II. Where do you need to be alert?

___

III. Who do you need to be watchful of?

___

IV. How can you develop your habits of being alert?

___

Safety Summary Answers

When to be alert:
    At night
    During the day
    Anytime

Where to be alert:
    In shopping centers
    In parking lots
    In your car
    Entering or leaving your home
    Everywhere

Who to watch for:
> Strangers who appear to be watching you
> Strangers who move into your space or territory without your permission
> People who are friends of your friends/spouse/family, whom you do not know well
> Anyone who makes you feel uncomfortable
> **Anyone**

How to be alert:
> Look right, left, in front and behind
> Watch for hiding places between parked cars
> Watch for hiding places in doorways or alley entrances
> Watch for hiding places
> Look for anything that appears out of place or wrong

Identify the missing safety habits in the following examples:

Christmas shopping was always a problem for Marge. She waited until the last minute this year as usual. She still had one more purchase to make and it was already 9:30, closing time. "Oh dear!", she thought to herself as she left the department store. "I'll have to buy Harold's present tomorrow. I thought I'd have all my shopping done tonight!" A saleswoman opened the door for her, then closed it and locked it. The saleswoman looked tired. She leaned against the door waiting for the other customers to leave. A last minute shopper hurried to the door and tried to get in. The saleswoman shook her head, and pointed to the locked door. She mouthed the word "Closed."

Marge shifted the packages in her arms, and looked at the parking lot. "Let's see," she thought, "I parked under a red rooster when I drove in this afternoon." She peered into the darkness. Snow was beginning to fall. Even though the parking lot was lit, the night seemed dark. Three red rooster signs were visible from the door. "Which one did I park my car next to?" Marge pondered. "I think it was that one," she thought as she walked diagonally across the lot toward the first sign. The car was not there. Her navy pinto was nestled in the falling snow next to the second red rooster sign.

She piled her packages and purse on the hood of the car as she began digging through her coat pockets to find her key. Finally she picked up her purse. After some shifting of the contents, she found the keys buried on the bottom. She opened the hatchback, then walked to the front of the car to pick up the packages still resting on the car hood. Then she piled the packages inside. She closed the hatch and then opened the car door, crawled in, and put her purse on the seat next to her. She left her car door ajar as she looked for her snow brush. By now the car was covered in snow. She brushed the snow from the car with her gloved hand and mentally made a note to buy a new snow brush and scraper. When she'd brushed the snow from the windows, she got back into the car, closed the door, started the car and headed for home. She sighed and thought, "What a day! At least now I can relax!"

Although Marge may sound like a typical Christmas shopper, she made some crucial safety errors.

How many can you identify? _____

_____
_____
_____
_____
_____
_____

Dick hated getting groceries. His wife always did this loathsome chore, until last March when the divorce was final. Then he'd found himself in a one bedroom apartment spending weekends getting groceries, washing laundry, and cleaning. He was thinking of hiring a maid service.

"I'll have my secretary find me a good maid service on Monday," he decided as he parked his car in the underground garage.

SAFETY: A HABIT

He opened the trunk and glared at the six grocery bags. "If I take three at a time, it will only take me two trips," he thought. He picked up two bags, one in each arm. He bent over and squashed the third bag in the middle between the two he held. The third bag was lower then the first two, so he lifted his knee, and let up enough on the pressure to center the third bag.

"Stupid door," he growled. The security door blocked his entry into the apartment lobby. Balancing the three bags with one arm and one knee, he managed to extract his key from his coat pocket. Each time he reached forward to place the key in the lock his grocery bags began to slip.

"May I help you?" a stranger inquired from his right.

"Please," responded Dick. "These security doors are such a nuisance. They really don't keep anyone out, you know."

The stranger reached out, took Dick's key and held open the door.

"Say, don't you have your own key?" Dick asked as the stranger returned the key.

"Oh I don't live here," replied the stranger, "I'm visiting a friend."

"Thanks," said Dick as he headed for the elevator. At the door to his apartment Dick repeated his earlier balancing performance. In exasperation he finally set the bags on the floor and opened the door. Then he grabbed a grocery bag in each arm and pushed the third bag into his apartment with his foot. When he left his apartment he propped a magazine in the door, and thought to himself, "When I come back with the last three bags, I'll get inside without the hassle." He took an extra magazine with him for the security door.

Dick may represent many apartment dwellers. What were his safety errors? _____

Her plane was delayed two hours in Chicago. By the time Shirley reached Minneapolis, it was dark. Getting her luggage and a taxi took another hour. By the time she checked into her hotel it was 9:15. She was hungry and tired. Her last meal had been nine hours ago.

The front desk clerk handed her a room key. "Your room is 420," he said. "I'm sorry there is nobody on duty after 9:00 to help with luggage. If you'll look at this map, I'll explain how to get to your room."

As she walked to the elevator, she thought, "I need two hours to prepare for my 8:30 appointment tomorrow. This night's work has just begun." The elevator door was closing, "Wait," Shirley called. The doors closed, then slowly opened.

"You almost missed it," said the man at the control panel. His smile never reached her eyes as they moved over Shirley.

"Thank you for waiting," she said as she sat her luggage next to the elevator wall, "will you push 4 please?"

Shirley finally reached room 420. Directly across the hall was 419. The door to 419 was ajar and the 9:00 news broadcasted into the hall. She started to open her door as a man stepped out of 419.

"Good evening," he said.

"Evening," she responded. The lock stuck. She tried to turn it, but nothing happened.

"Need some help?" he asked. She turned the key the other way and the door opened. She smiled to herself. "No thank you. I was just turning the key the wrong way," she laughed.

Identify the safety mistakes Shirley made. _____

_____

_____

_____

_____

_____

_____

_____

_____

Marge's Safety Mistakes

1) Marge was rushed. When people rush they often forget common safety habits such as locking car doors.

2) Marge had her hands occupied with packages. A shopping bag with handles may free her hands or she could take the packages to her car at intervals while she shops. She could even check on package delivery.

3) The store is locked. Marge has NO where safe to run if she meets trouble in the parking lot.

4) Marge forgot where she parked her car.

5) Marge is a good victim target when she piles her purse and packages on the car to look for car keys. She should have had her keys in her hand before she left the store.

6) She leaves her car door ajar with her purse on the seat. She should close the car door and put her purse on the floor.

7) She did not lock her car when she left it in the parking lot. She did not lock the car when she got in and started home. She did not check the back seat to see if anyone was hiding.

Dick's Safety Mistakes

1) Dick had his arms full. He needs to take fewer bags to keep his hands free.

2) Dick not only ruined his security system but also the security of others in his apartment building when he allowed the stranger to use his key. Dick left his apartment door unlocked and ajar.

3) Many people do not lock their doors when unloading items from their car. An unlocked house or apartment, even for a second, is an invitation for a thief.

Shirley's Safety Mistakes

1) Shirley is tired and hungry. This may present vulnerable nonverbal behavior to a potential attacker. Shirley needs to carry something to eat while she is traveling to fight the image of a "tired, hungry" target. When tired and hungry, most people loose their alertness for potentially dangerous situations.

2) Shirley needed to insist on an escort to her room.

3) She is thinking about her appointment tomorrow. Not focusing her awareness on her safety is a big mistake.

4) Shirley should have waited for the next elevator. She put herself in a potentially dangerous situation: no one on duty at the desk, no people available for help, alone on an elevator with a potential attacker and feeling tired and hungry.

5) The door ajar to 419 should have been a clue for Shirley. When a man stepped into the hall, Shirley should have immediately started back to the front desk and not opened her door.

6) When Shirley opened the door to her room she was a prime target. She could have easily been pushed into her room by the man in the hall. Once in her room with an attacker, she would have drastically cut down her available escape options.

Shirley, Dick and Marge, have one big mistake in common. They were not alert to potentially dangerous situations. Developing healthy awareness is much like enjoying a pleasant walk. During the walk, you notice trees, other people walking, and a stray dog. Shirley, Dick and Marge needed the same type of alertness to notice their environments.

6
Decisions: What to do and when to do it.

You've followed all the safety guidelines. Your car is parked in a parking lot under a street light. You worked late. It's dark. Everyone has gone home. You head for the parking lot. Your keys are in your hand. He materializes out of nowhere and suddenly you know "this is it." This is a dangerous situation. What should you do? You need to make a decision quickly.

To make a decision in this situation, it is important to understand how we make decisions. Each decision we make involves our total experience of existence, our whole being. Whenever a decision is made many factors influence what we finally decide. Factors such as: past and present experiences, value systems, beliefs, intuition, prevailing emotions, facts, health, physical energy, current pressures, and perception of the situation. All of these factors and others play a part in the decision of what to do in a dangerous situation. There is no right, single answer. There are many choices. Each individual has the responsibility to make the right decision for him or herself. Four factors effect the quality of the decision; awareness, understanding, wisdom and training. In every dangerous situation, it is important to recognize that individuals are already making their best decision, not necessarily **the** best decision. Each individual uses all his/her experiences, values, beliefs, mental accumulation of knowledge, etc., to come up with the best choice he/she can make. People learn to make better decisions with awareness, more understanding of what alternatives are available, and training in what to do and how to do it. All this adds up to wisdom. The wisdom to know what decision to make and when to make it.

In the decision making process model (figure 3), eight elements effect the decision you make in any potentially dangerous situation. All of these elements together make up the sum total of your experience and existence. Although this book will not change your existence, it may help you look at your experiences and understand your ability or inability to make certain decisions in threatening situations.

THE DECISION MAKING PROCESS

Elements That Affect Decision Making	The Decision	Elements That Increase Effective Decision Making
Prevailing emotions	All elements become fixed at the point in time of the decision	Awareness
Past and present experiences		Understanding
Personal values		Training
Belief systems and attitudes		Wisdom
Current environmental pressures		
Social conditioning		
Factual knowledge of the situation		
Mental accumulation of all knowledge		

FIGURE 3

The first element that affects your decision making is prevailing emotions. The next two stories are examples of prevailing emotions affecting decision making.

Frank just finished a meeting with his manager, where he'd been unjustly accused of taking long lunches. He hid his feelings for the rest of the day, but at four o'clock when he left the office he was angry. He slammed the door as he walked out of the office building, and strode to his car. A young tough approached Frank as he got into his car and told him to hand over his wallet. This was the straw that broke the camel's back. Frank's anger increased threefold. He bellowed like a bull as he leaped out of his car and took after the youth. The youth sped away as quickly as his feet would carry him. In this case Frank's prevailing emotion, righteous anger, may have helped him survive. In other situations, his righteous anger may have gotten him into trouble.

After working overtime in a grueling job as waitress, Sally left work dog tired. As she started toward her car, she realized the street light was out again. Out of the shadows appeared a large man. Sally was so tired, she looked at him, shook her head and kept walking. She physically did not have the energy to be frightened. The man stared at her, yelled a few obscenities and walked by.

In both cases, prevailing emotions helped the individuals remain safe in potentially dangerous situations. This isn't necessarily true in every situation. If your prevailing emotion is defeat, fear or arrogance, a dangerous situation may escalate. Be aware of your prevailing emotions, and maintain the emotional flexibility to react to perilous situations.

The second element that affects decision making is; past and present experiences. Your life experiences effect how you deal with dangerous situations. For example, many people believe people are proper and courteous. Believing people are proper and courteous is a nice belief. It is also a belief that may get you deeper in trouble. Often an aggressor will stalk his victim by asking, "Do you have the time?" He expects the victim to respond courteously. Maybe you're one of the lucky people who has never had anyone try to hurt or threaten you. Because of this you have a basic belief that people are kind and good. This belief may stop you from recognizing a dangerous situation. It is possible to remain alert and still believe that the majority of people are kind and worth your trust.

Your personal values will also effect your decisions. Self image is part of your personal value system. If you have a high self image you may believe, "I'm worthwhile, and no one has the right to do anything to me without my permission." The value you place on yourself, may help you survive a threatening situation. If on the other hand, you have low self esteem and do not value your worth as a person, this may effect your decision when you are confronted.

Current environmental pressures may also effect your decision making process. Perhaps you are under a great deal of stress, or you may feel overworked and tired, or you may be merely walking down a street deep in thought about a business problem. These types of pressures may allow you to slack off your awareness and become a target.

Social conditioning too may play a large factor in the decision you make in a threatening situation. Many people have been socially conditioned to be polite, to wait their turn, to only take their share, to say excuse me, to keep their voice low and well modulated, and be courteous to all.

One reported situation of this social conditioning occurred when a young man approached a woman and asked directions. She was polite and told him she couldn't help him. He continued walking with her and put his hand at her elbow. She was conditioned to be polite. In her own words; "I didn't want him to think I considered him aggressive." She made a slight shrug of her shoulders to let him know his advances weren't appreciated. When he put his arm around her she said in her quiet, well modulated voice, "Please stop." He forced her into the alley and raped her. There were many decisions she could have made to remain safe, but her social conditioning of being polite in all situations set her up as a target.

Your factual knowledge of any situation is extremely important. Know your environment! If you're walking downtown do you know which businesses are open? Do you know where people are available so you can call for help? Are you meeting someone? In addition to environmental knowledge, it's also important to have knowledge about your self defense abilities.

Decisions can be reactive or proactive. The reactive decision is when you decide to react to the situation as you perceive it. The proactive action is perceiving a developing dangerous situation and taking action before the aggressor does. A proactive action could be staying in your car because someone looks suspicious, or waiting for the next elevator because you didn't feel right about the people in the first elevator. There is a range of reactive and proactive actions which can be taken in any situation.

In any situation where you need clear concise decisions define the limits of the situations. Determine what the problem is, and is not and watch for decision making roadblocks such as;

1. Lack of planning
2. Lack of a strategy
3. Lack of a clear goal
4. Lack of a clear understanding of the situation
5. Lack of critical skills to survive the situation
6. Lack of timing
7. Lack of appropriate action to reduce the conflict

To make effective decisions develop an awareness of potentially dangerous situations and an understanding of those elements which hinder or help your decision making. Understanding ourselves, our prevailing emotions, our present and past experiences, our beliefs system and attitudes, common decision making roadblocks and our social conditioning, will increase our ability to make effective decisions.

7
Survival Alternatives

There are many alternatives in every situation. Wisdom is the ability to quickly determine the alternatives and make the best decision you can. "What are the alternatives?" and "How does one decide which alternative to use?", are two questions to consider carefully. The first step in making an effective decision is identification, **recognizing the problem**. To quickly identify the specific problem, try asking yourself questions to direct your attention focus to the problem. Questions such as: "What's wrong?", "What is the magnitude of the problem?", "What is the environment?". These questions help the individual define and clarify an accurate perception of the situation.

....Your keys are in your hand. He materializes out of nowhere and suddenly you know "this is it."

You think
What's wrong?

Your answer
1. The man appears to be menacing. He's coming near you.
2. The parking lot is empty.

What's the environment?	1. The man is between you and your car. 2. The building is 20 feet behind you, locked. 3. The security guard is gone for the night.
What is the magnitude of the problem?	1. Since the magnitude of the problem is unknown at this point in time, assume extreme caution.

The entire process of problem identification will only take seconds. These are your most valuable seconds as this short pause will help you gather information that may save your life.

The second step in seeking a solution is to **determine your alternatives**. The range of alternatives varies from insane behavior to attacking. Consider your full range of alternatives before a dangerous situation occurs. Figure 4 is a visual representation of the range of alternatives available in many situations.

The numbers 1 through 6 on the vertical axis of the graph represent physical alternatives that could be used in certain situations. The categories are not meant to represent clear cut physical boundaries of behavior. Rather they are indicative of a range of physical behaviors that could work depending on the situation. The range of behaviors is not meant to be inclusive or exclusive. There may be other physical behaviors that might work for you. The vertical axis serves only as a reminder that many physical alternatives are available for us to choose from if necessary.

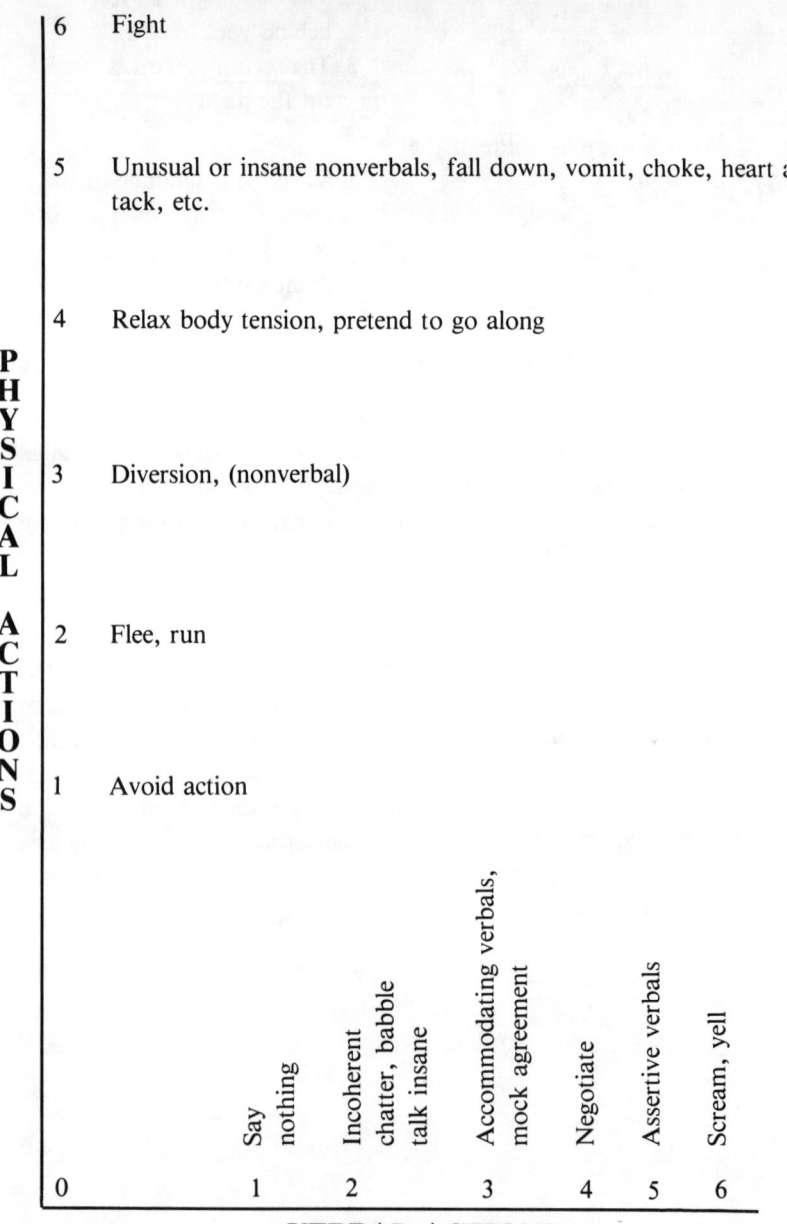

FIGURE 4
GRID OF ALTERNATIVES

A brief description of the physical alternatives is as follows; (The numbers next to the actions correspond to the numbers on the vertical axis from figure 4.)

Physical Alternatives

1. **Avoid action.** Depending on the situation, taking no action may be your best decision. If you walk into your home and a burglar waves a gun and shouts, "Don't move or I'll shoot!" your best alternative is to freeze. If you find yourself being harrassed verbally as you walk down a street, the best action may be to take no action. Ignore the comments and keep walking.

2. **Flee, run.** Running for your life may be your best decision if you have a safe place to run to. Run toward safety. Safe areas may include public areas with other people around, or well lit areas where other people can see your plight. Fleeing may not be the best decision if you have no safe place to go. Running away from danger will merely physically tire you and leave you less able to deal with the situation if there's no where to run.

3. **Diversion.** Diversion may be your best decision if you choose to confuse or muddle you aggressor's thoughts. Diversion is the attempt to redirect your aggressor so that he focuses his attention on something or someone else. Any physical action that surprises or diverts the attention of your assailant may be an effective physical diversion. A simple diversion is to pretend to be waiting for someone. Look at your watch. Glance up and down the street. Tap your foot, etc. That small diversion may be enough to tell a would be assailant that you're expecting someone any second.

4. **Relax body tension, pretend to go along.** Pretending to go along with an aggressor can buy time and place you in an advantageous position to use another alternative later. If someone sneaks up behind you and lifts you off the ground pinning your arms in a bear hug, relaxing your body may cause the attacker to put you down. When you are released you have many other alternatives open to you. If an attacker pushes you toward his car, you may want to move with him at first, and then use the momentum to quickly spin away from him. If you suddenly move with your attacker, he may be caught off guard or relax his hold on you.

5. **Insane nonverbals.** Often an aggressor has a specific script he wants his victim to follow. When a victim doesn't follow the script, the aggressor may not continue the aggression. Behaviors such as faking a heart attack may frighten an aggressor away. The penalty for injuring someone during a crime is usually greater if he is caught and prosecuted. Falling down, hitting yourself, feigning insanity, vomiting, choking, are behaviors that may frighten an aggressor away.

6. **Fight back.** Survival is a basic motivation for all living creatures. You have the right to fight for your safety and survival. You are not in a boxing contest to determine a winner or loser. There are no "fair rules." You must be prepared to fight dirty and use the force necessary to insure your safety. You must be determined, more determined than your attacker. Your two greatest assets are your determination and commitment to do anything you must to insure your safety and survival.

The verbal range of alternatives is represented in figure 4 by the horizontal axis 1-6. The verbal alternatives are neither inclusive nor exclusive of all the verbal actions that could be effectively used in a dangerous situation. The horizontal axis is a reminder that many verbal alternatives are available. A brief description of the verbal alternatives is as follows; (The numbers next to the verbal alternatives correspond to the numbers on the horizontal axis from figure 4.)

Verbal Alternatives

1. **Say nothing.** Saying nothing can be a good strategy depending on the situation. Silence doesn't mean you are weak or passive. It can be used as a good way to assess the situation while you watch for alternatives. "Silence is golden," may be most true when you're confronted by someone under the influence of alcohol or drugs. Anything you say may agitate him.

2. **Incoherent chatter, babble, talk insane.** The aggressor desperately needs a victim to play a part. To verbally break the aggressor's script of how the situation should turn out, the victim may decide to talk gibberish, roll his/her eyes, let his/her tongue hangout. This may cause the aggressor to hesitate and allow the victim to get away or plan another alternative.

3. **Accommodating verbals, mock agreement.** Let the aggressor think you have the same goals as he does. Pretend to agree with him and be on his side. Psychologically, this handicaps the aggressor because the "Me vs. You" has turned into "Us and We." Someone breaks into your home and threatens rape. You reply, "Let's get into something more comfortable and have a drink first. You get the Vodka and ice and I'll get more comfortable." Then you lock yourself in your bedroom and call the police or choose another alternative. The whole point is to agree with your aggressor so that you develop the advantage.

4. **Negotiate.** Talk to your attacker. Communicate as an equal. Don't beg or plead. Stay calm. You might say to a robber, "Listen, I don't want you to get hurt. I realize with the economy the way it is everyone has to eat. So take what you need and hurry. My roommate is a cop and he frequently stops in around this time for coffee."

    There's the famous Alexander Dumas' story of Jean Valjean, the thief who stole the golden candlesticks from a priest. When Jean was caught the priest told him to take the candlesticks and anything else he wanted, because he needed them more than the church. Jean was so amazed by the unusual behavior of the priest, that he turned his life away from crime and became an exemplary citizen.

5. **Assertive verbals.** The assertive person is a person who has a strong sense of "I am." He/she knows he/she is valuable and recognizes that value. He/she is able to express his/her thoughts and feelings. Just as people have social conditioning to a policeman holding up his hand saying. "Stop," many people are conditioned to certain words such as; "Stop," "Leave me alone." Such words said with force and conviction may stop an aggressor or buy you time to get an advantage.

6. **Scream, yell.** Especially if people are near enough to hear you, screaming and yelling may be the action you choose. Most attackers don't want a crowd. The right scream or yell may bring people or scare your attacker away. Many people suggest screaming "Fire" instead of just screaming or screaming for help. "Fire" seems to bring others to your aid fastest.

Depending on the situation any of the alternatives can work. Whether the alternative works and saves you from a dangerous situation, depends on your, believability. Believability is developed through thinking out your choices and taking the time to practice them mentally or physically. If you've thought through your alternatives, and have taken time to plan them, with the extra adrenalin in the real situation you have a very good opportunity to be believable. Each one of the alternatives listed in the alternative grid has been used successfully at some time by individuals to keep themselves safe, secure and alive in dangerous situations.

The following are true stories collected over a three year period. They occurred in Minnesota, Washington D.C., New York, Montana, California, Florida and Alabama. My sincere thanks to all those people who supplied me with real life situations of survival.

It was late at night. He was on a dimly lit street. He'd been studying for final exams at a friend's apartment late into the night. He had a mile to walk before he reached his own small walk-up apartment and the neighborhood was known for its high crime rate. Out of the shadows across the street, two men appeared. They cut diagonally across the street and moved toward him menacingly. He stopped walking. He took a deep breath and as he stood there he systematically relaxed his body. He relaxed his facial muscles. He relaxed his arms. He neither looked at the men nor away from them. He looked neither aggressive nor defensive. He stood in a relaxed posture and waited. He was the total picture of awareness and expectation. The two men strode up and stopped on either side of him. The silence deepened. No one said anything. Finally one of the two said, "Ah, let's go find somebody else."

In this case the potential victim did not play the script. He did not ask, "What do you want?" He did not say, "Don't hurt me." He merely stood, relaxed his body and waited. In this unique situation, the alternative seemed to be a good choice. As the potential victim had many hours of marial art's training, he had other choices. None of the alternatives will work 100 percent of the time. In this situation, however, it appeared to be a wise choice to do nothing and to say nothing. It is easy to determine a wise choice. The wise choice results in keeping you safe and alive.

He was in a metropolitan city. The taxis were on strike, so he caught a subway. The subway car was empty. Empty paper bags and newspapers scattered over the seats were left from the afternoon commuter rush. He cleared away some papers and sat down. It had been a long, long day, and he was tired. The subway train screeched to a halt. He looked up as movement caught his eye. Three young men strutted into the subway car. A skull and crossbones was stenciled on their jackets. They seemed to wear their jeans and jackets like uniforms. The tallest youth with dark curly hair glanced at the commuter sitting alone. He stopped chewing his gum and gave a low wolf whistle. "Well, well," he said as he nudged one of his friends in the ribs. "Lookit over there." All three youths sauntered over and stood in front of the commuter. No one said anything as the youths appraised the man. He was dressed in a dark suit and button down shirt. A tie was neatly knotted at his throat, and in his hand he held a briefcase. The black haired youth stood in front of him, legs far apart, his hands on his hips. He leaned forward at the waist and said, "Hey man, you got some money?" The man looked at the youth and responded, "Quelle? Escaque."

"What'd you say?" responded the youth. The man continued with a torrent of syllables sounding like no language the youth had ever heard. The dark haired youth glanced at his two companions.

Did you understand what he said?" he asked. Both boys shook their heads no. The second youth, a boy with straight, stringy blond hair said, "Hey man, you let me try." He turned to the businessman and threatened, "Man, you give us money, or we cut you." The businessman cocked his head to the side as if listening. Then a light of recognition flashed in his eyes. He nodded his head, jumped up, smiled, slapped the boy on the back, shook his hand, and said, "Es Ce Que Vo Sou..." The black haired leader struck his friend and hissed, "You stupid, you can't threaten someone who can't understand you." He glanced at both of his partners in disgust, shrugged his shoulders and said, "Ah, let's get out of here. Can't stand sharing a car with a foreigner."

In this situation the potential victim chose to speak jibberish. He chose to pretend he could not understand. He made that choice when he saw the youths walk through the door. When he assessed the situation he determined the youths were inexperienced. Their manhood was important to them so if pushed they would probably fight. At the same time he realized all three were very much afraid. By choosing this alternative he remained safe and alive. He could have chosen another alternative. Other alternatives may have worked, but in his wisdom, this alternative appeared to be the best one for him in this situation. It is interesting to note that the individual in this situation had hundreds of hours of martial arts training. Often people who know they have the alternative of fighting as a last resort, have the confidence to try other alternatives.

"Come to the party, you'll have a great time," said her friend. That had been five hours ago and her friend Monica was right. Monica was having a great time. They'd been at the party less then fifteen minutes before Monica disappeared with the tall good looking man. After Monica disappeared, she'd wandered through the house talking to different people. Most of them were pretty strange. One man was really beginning to bother her. Every time she turned around, he seemed to be staring at her. All she wanted to do was to go home, but Monica had the keys to the car. Her eyes swept the room looking for Monica's short blond hair. She saw a blond leaving the house. She threaded past people toward the door. When she got to the door the blond was gone. She thought to herself, "You don't suppose that little twerp left me here?" She walked out of the door to see if the car was still in the parking lot. The night was cool and felt good against her skin. She walked down the steps and peered around the corner looking for the yellow Firebird. The Firebird was still there. "Monica must be inside," she thought. She turned to go back. A hand reached out and grabbed her shoulder. A voice said, "You're coming with me." She looked into the face of the man who'd been watching her all night and felt a shiver run down her spine. She smiled sweetly and said, "Oh, I'm so glad you found me, I walked out here hoping you'd follow me. I've been watching you all night and waiting to talk to you. Let's get away from this loud, noisy party so we can be alone." The grip on her shoulder loosened.

"You're coming with me," he said again.

"Well of course I'm coming with you," she replied. "I've been hoping you'd ask me all night. All I have to do is get my coat. It's chilly out here. Do you have a car?" she asked. He nodded, still suspicious.

"Why don't you get your car and I'll get my coat. I'll meet you right in front in about 30 seconds. Okay?" He nodded and started toward the parking lot.

Our potential victim in this situation chose mock agreement as a means of removing herself from a potentially dangerous situation. Of course she had other alternatives, but the alternative she chose seemed to be the best alternative for her in this situation.

Your voice may be your best alternative, as in the case of the professional singer. She had remarkable vocal control and a vocal range that easily hit the upper register. So when he grabbed her in a crowded airport and growled, "Come with me," she dropped all her baggage, took a huge breath and hit an upper E flat. He fled as fast as he could. The sound was so piercing and intense, almost everyone in the airport turned and looked.

In this situation her best alternative was her voice. In the following account, verbal alternatives may have been the worst choice.

He was at a convention. He traveled frequently and was comfortable with motel living. Some conventioneers were in the lobby, while others filed into the banquet hall. He checked his coat pocket and discovered he'd left his banquet tickets in his room upstairs. He boarded the empty elevator, and noticed the third floor button was pushed. "That's odd," he thought to himself, "there's no one on the elevator and yet the third floor button is lit. Probably some kids." On the third floor a man dressed in a three piece suit got on the elevator and walked to the back wall. The conventioneer stood near the buttons, "Which floor do you want?" he asked. Suddenly a gun appeared in the stranger's hand. "I don't want a floor," he said. "I just want your money." The conventioneer remained silent. "Just ease your wallet out of your pocket," said the stranger. "Hand it over very carefully." The conventioneer slowly and deliberately reached into his pocket, removed his wallet and handed it to the stranger. "Now, don't do anything stupid," said the stranger as he pushed the button for the twelfth floor. As the elevator doors opened on the twelfth floor the stranger said, "Get out here." The conventioneer walked out the door. When he turned around the door had closed. Throughout the process he had said nothing. He lost some fifty dollars in money, but he was safe and alive. The conventioneer's wisdom told him his best decision was to do nothing. The money could be replaced, but his life could not. The conventioneer judged the situation to be dangerous. He perceived the stranger to be a professional. The robber knew the elevator would stop at floor three. He had chose his target carefully. His timing was flawless, the whole experience took less than two minutes. As the conventioneer thought over the situation, he nodded grimly to himself and thought, "Yes I made the best decision."

In Bloomington, Minnesota, there's a jogger who saved her life by running. She chose to flee. An avid jogger, she was up bright and early to jog around the lake. She had the same routine. Each morning she jogged four miles, showered, ate breakfast and caught a bus to work in downtown Minneapolis. It was a beautiful July morning as she limbered her hamstrings, and began to jog slowly. She jogged about a mile around the south end of the lake, and was headed north when a man jumped out from behind a tree and tried to grab her. She used her body momentum to break his grip. Then she ran as fast as she could east. The attacker followed. Several times he moved to intercept her, but each time she was able to break away with a burst of speed. "Only a block to go," she thought to herself. She ran the last block as if her life depended on it, and it probably did. She was able to stay out of range of her attacker for the last block. Lungs burning she spotted two men walking down the steps at the building she was running toward. She crossed the last 20 yards waving her arms, and planted herself in front of their squad car. Her attacker, now winded, gazed confusedly around. The two officers jumped out of their car and apprehended the culprit. She made a wise choice. Our avid jogger ran to the police station. In the early morning hours with no one around to help her, she made her best decision. She ran for her life. She chose wisely as she had a place to run to. She knew her territory and the location of the police station. She had other alternatives. She chose the best one for her situation, and that was to flee.

Another jogger tells this story:

Because she frequently worked odd hours, she chose to jog whenever she could. One early morning she was jogging around the perimeter of a shopping center. It was still dark and the sun was many hours away. As a marathon runner she trained rigorously. This morning she planned to run 15 miles. A pickup began to pace her as she ran.

She assessed the situation. She had put herself in an extremely dangerous situation. It was one o'clock in the morning. There was no one around. She was on the perimeter road of a shopping center and a man in a pickup was pacing her. The pickup stopped. A light haired man got out and walked toward her. She stopped jogging and caught her breath. She spoke first. "Hey, I don't know what you're up to, but let me tell you something. Only a fool would come to a shopping center and jog at one o'clock in the morning. I'm no fool, my husband is a cop and picks me up here. In fact he makes his round about now. He dropped me off about half an hour ago and he's scheduled to report here in five minutes. I also know Karate. I believe I know enough to keep you occupied for the five minutes it'll take my husband to get here. So if you want trouble, just stick around," she said as she stepped into her Karate stance. The man turned around, walked to the pickup, got in and drove away. She had effectively used a diversion. When the man got out of his pickup, she looked at her watch and checked the time. This told the would be attacker, nonverbally that she was waiting for someone. Then she glanced up and down the perimeter road as if she was expecting someone. Both of these diversionary nonverbals aided her believability when she told her story.

It was a wintry Sunday afternoon. The washing machine at home wasn't working so she volunteered to do the family laundry at the local laundromat. It was twilight as she finished the last load of laundry and folded it into the yellow basket. "It will take two trips to get it out to the car," she thought. She hoisted the yellow basket onto her hip and walked toward the door. She balanced the basket on her hip, reached forward with her hand and pulled open the door. The cold air rushed into the room, she shivered, propped the door open with her foot and heaved the basket through the open door. She was almost to her car when he grabbed her wrist. His grip seemed like iron as he pulled her toward him. The basket fell and she struggled against the grip. The harder she struggled the tighter he held her wrist. Suddenly she stopped struggling and walked toward him. Immediately the pressure on her wrist decreased. She relaxed her arm and allowed the entire hand to go limp. The pressure on her wrist decreased even more. Then with a sudden jerk she broke his grip by pulling her wrist away from his thumb. She pivoted on her feet, ran around to the passenger side of her car, jumped in and locked the door. Her laundry was scattered all over the sidewalk, but she was safe and alive inside her car. She started the engine and drove to the nearest police station. She chose to relax her body and allow her wrist and arm to go limp, thus causing the attacker to loosen his painful grip. When the attacker thought she'd given in, he let up the pressure. This choice took a split second. Her movement took a split second. The entire confrontation lasted less then 10 seconds. In that brief period of time she made a decision. Her decision was to relax her body until the right time to break away. She had other alternatives; this one worked for her as she is safe and alive.

She was walking home from work when the car stopped. The passenger door opened, a man dressed in sweat gear leaped out and grabbed her. Before she could use an alternative he dragged her into the car. At this point she quickly made a decision. She stuck her finger down her throat and vomited over her attacker and the car. Then she gasped, "I've got the flu. I think I'm going to be sick again." The driver slammed on his brakes and yelled at his friend, "Get that _____ broad out of this car." Uncerimoniously she was dumped in the street. She chose an unusual alternative. She considered her options carefully and chose the alternative she knew would be most convincing, and it worked. When the situation was over, she was safe and unharmed. (When I first heard this story I expressed disbelief, but was assured by her Doctor husband that his wife had such a gag reflex that she frequently vomited on a moment's notice.)

She was traveling on business. She'd covered her entire five hundred miles sales territory. For ten hours she'd been driving. Exhausted, she finally stopped at a roadside motel and checked in. She fell into bed and immediately slept a deep restful sleep. Her attacker came through the bathroom window. She awakened when he placed two hands against her shoulders holding her flat on the bed. She immediately slammed the heel of her hand into his nose. He stumbled back. She threw off the covers and leaped up. The heel of her foot stomped his instep then his knee. He grabbed his knee as he fell to the floor. She picked up the lamp, smashed him over the head, grabbed her car keys and fled to her car, where she honked the horn until she had awakened most of the motel guests and the motel owner. She had been alone in her room with no help, and she chose to fight. She was 100 percent committed to her alternative. She did not have to win or score points. She survived unharmed.

These and many other stories are common stories of potential victims who managed to keep themselves safe and unharmed. All of the potential victims have some qualities in common. First their decision making ability. Each potential victim made a decision to remain safe and unharmed. Each chose an alternative that helped them survive unharmed. In each situation the potential victims chose their alternatives recognizing they had others to choose from if the first choice didn't work. The grid of alternatives was designed to show many of the choices available. If you use the horizontal and vertical axis as pairs, you will see the many combinations available.

A list of alternatives follows:
1. Say nothing
2. Do nothing
3. Say nothing and do nothing
4. Flee
5. Use a diversion
6. Use an unusual nonverbal
7. Fight
8. Chatter, use jibberish
9. Babble jibberish as you run away
10. Babble jibberish and use diversion
11. Babble jibberish as you fake an unusual nonverbal such as vomiting or heart attack
12. Babble jibberish as you fight
13. Pretend to agree
14. Pretend to agree while you prepare to run away
15. Pretend to agree while you use a diversion such as looking at your watch or looking up and down the street
16. Pretend to agree while you choose an unusual behavior
17. Pretend to agree, then fight
18. Use assertive nonverbals
19. Use assertive nonverbals then run
20. Use assertive nonverbals as you prepare a diversion
21. Use assertive nonverbals while you exhibit an unusual behavior
22. Use assertive nonverbals while you fight
23. Scream and yell while you run
24. Scream and yell while you create a diversion

25. Scream and yell while you use an unusual nonverbal behavior
26. Scream and yell as you fight

Which alternatives do you believe that you could use convincingly?

___
___
___
___
___
___
___

What guidelines would you use to determine when you would use which alternative?

Example: I will run if I have somewhere to run to.

___
___
___
___
___
___
___
___
___

SURVIVAL ALTERNATIVES

It's important to understand when to choose a different alternative. If you choose an alternative and it doesn't work, be very careful of "getting stuck" or continuing to use the same alternative. If an alternative doesn't work, chose another. For example: A potential victim chooses to yell and scream. The attacker grabs the victim who continues to yell and scream. No one comes to the victim's aid. The attacker begins to beat the victim. The more the victim screams, the more he beats her. If this occurs, stop screaming and try another alternative. You have some 25 alternatives to choose from. A victim often chooses an alternative that doesn't work and then continues to use the alternative that's not working. Your behavior flexibility or your ability to choose different alternatives may save your life.

To identify the alternatives which are acceptable to you, read through the following list. Place a star by those alternatives you believe you could choose. Place an X by those alternatives which are not acceptable to you. Be sure to add any other alternatives that come to mind.

_____ 1. Say nothing
_____ 2. Do nothing
_____ 3. Say nothing and do nothing
_____ 4. Flee
_____ 5. Use a diversion
_____ 6. Use an unusual nonverbal
_____ 7. Fight
_____ 8. Chatter, use jibberish
_____ 9. Babble jibberish as you run away
_____10. Babble jibberish and use diversion
_____11. Babble jibberish as you fake an unusual nonverbal such as vomiting or heart attack
_____12. Babble jibberish as you fight
_____13. Pretend to agree
_____14. Pretend to agree while you prepare to run away
_____15. Pretend to agree while you use a diversion such as looking at your watch or looking up and down the street
_____16. Pretend to agree while you choose an unusual behavior
_____17. Pretend to agree, then fight
_____18. Use assertive nonverbals

_____19. Use assertive nonverbals then run
_____20. Use assertive nonverbals as you prepare a diversion
_____21. Use assertive nonverbals while you exhibit an unusual behavior
_____22. Use assertive nonverbals while you fight
_____23. Scream and yell while you run
_____24. Scream and yell while you create a diversion
_____25. Scream and yell while you use an unusual nonverbal behavior
_____26. Scream and yell as you fight

Others: _____

_____

_____

If you checked some of the alternatives as not acceptable, please go back and consider them again. Is there some decision making element that stops you from using those alternatives? Have you had an experience which stops you from using those alternatives or do you have a personal belief system that interferes with choosing them? Identify what stops you from accepting the checked alternatives as viable in the right situation. List the unacceptable alternatives and explain your reasons for not choosing them.

Alternatives I would not use

1. _____

   _____

   _____

2. _____

   _____

   _____

   _____

3. _____

Reasons I would not choose these alternatives

1. _____

2. _____

3. _____

From the list of alternatives you have starred choose three alternatives that you would be most comfortable using. List them below next to numbers 1, 2 and 3. For each alternative, consider your background, situations when the alternative would be appropriate, situations when the alternative would not be appropriate, and any factors that might hinder your use of the alternative.

(SAMPLE)

Alternative	Background Data	Appropriate Situations	Inappropriate Situations	Hindering factors
1. Fight	I've never had to fight.	When life is in danger	"Minor" confrontation, no physical danger	I have no training in fighting.

Alternative	Background Data	Appropriate Situations	Inappropriate Situations	Hindering factors
	(Past experience with this alternative. Personal belief about this alternative. Any conditioning or training that would affect use of this alternative.)			
1. _____	_____	_____	_____	_____

SURVIVAL ALTERNATIVES

2. _____ _____ _____ _____ _____

3. _____ _____ _____ _____ _____

Developing an awareness of usable alternatives adds to your understanding of yourself and your available options. Remember the best alternative in any situation is the alternative that gets you maximum benefit or survival with minimum risk. There are many alternatives in every situation. To decide which alternative to use; carefully consider the total situation, determine your alternatives and use your wisdom to choose your action.

FIGURE 5

8
Just for Women

Women in the United States have freedom. They can leave their homes alone. They can attend a movie alone. They can frequent a bar alone. Yet there is another side to that freedom. Whenever a woman walks alone at night, enters a bar, or a movie theater alone, she violates a "well established" rule of conduct and as a result she faces the possibility of rape. The rule she violates can be stated: "A proper woman has an escort."

To add to this problem, if a woman is raped when she is alone at a bar, a movie or hitchhiking, the man will frequently escape prosecution. The woman will be made to feel that somehow she's responsible for the rape because she was asking for it. How was she asking for it? She violated the rule of conduct; proper women are expected to have an escort.

In the United States there are new freedoms and responsibilities for women. Women need to accept responsibility for keeping themselves safe, so they can appreciate their freedom. It's important for females to understand that "being female" make you a candidate for sexual assault. Every day women learn to accept that their freedom is limited in a way a man's freedom is not. A man has the right to go for a walk alone at night. If a woman goes for a walk alone at night the rules of conduct says she's asking to be a victim. If a woman is sexually assaulted the woman not the man, must have been walking in the wrong neighborhood, or wearing the wrong clothes, or out at the wrong time of day. The woman, not the man, must have been doing something wrong, otherwise she wouldn't have been raped.

It's amazing that rape is one of the few cases where the victim gets the responsibility for the crime. People often buy new cars, gold chains, jewelry, etc. When these items are stolen I've never heard anyone say, "Well if you hadn't purchased the expensive item it wouldn't have been stolen." In other words the blame for the theft is on the thief's shoulders. This is not true in the case of rape. Somehow in the case of rape the situation is turned around and the victim ends up with the responsibility for the crime. Therefore, if rape or sexual assault occurs, the woman is usually blamed. Regardless of the time of day, what she is wearing, or where she is, because she is female, a woman can be a victim.

Look at the statistics! Women are a large percentage of the victim population. It's time to take a long hard look at the facts:

- Approximately 1 out of 10 American women will be criminally sexually assaulted sometime in her life.
- Once every 10 minutes a woman is raped in the United States.
- Studies indicate that approximately 75 percent of the victims of sexual assaults are threatened with death or great bodily harm.
- Sexual assaults know no age limit.

These are just some of the statistics. They do not include other crimes such as burglary, purse snatching, robbery, mugging, etc. Women should not be lulled into a false sense of security. During the last decade women have been discovering new freedoms; careers with job mobility, travelling alone on business or pleasure, shopping alone, etc. All of these new freedoms add up to new responsibilities. In the past women often looked to men for protection. Today women have the freedom of not needing an escort, but they have the responsibility for their own safety. In this new age of continued freedom for women, many are not prepared for the responsibility of their own safety. The following three stories are examples of women who had freedom, sometimes without the responsibility.

Her name is Barbara. She has an excellent job with an equipment manufacturer. One of her duties is to coordinate demonstration shows. To organize the shows, Barbara flies in a week before the opening. Her assembly crew comes two days later to begin assembling the equipment. Barbara oversees the assemblage and coordinates the set up. When everything is ready, the trade show opens. Barbara stays with the show, selling and answering questions.

At one large convention center, she was one of twenty equipment dealers at the trade show. During the show several dealers hired curvacious young women in see-through blouses to pose around their equipment. During the setup and the week run, Barbara had the opportunity to meet many salesman from other companies working in jobs much like hers. On Friday the show closed. Barbara's crew requested to leave early and fly home for Friday evening. Barbara consented. She stayed to make sure everything was packed and crated. She planned a late flight out.

The engineers left on the 1 o'clock flight. Customers started leaving the convention center about 3:30. By 4:00 the customers were gone. Barbara and the fifteen other salesmen finished the last minute closing details. A few of the men began teasing Barbara. Several asked if she would go out for a drink with them. A few made lewd comments about her sexual abilities. Barbara felt uncomfortable. She finished closing and started to leave when someone blocked her exit. She knew she was in a dangerous position. A tall man from a nearby exhibit taunted, "You've been wiggling your behind in front of us for three days now, maybe it's time to take action." Another man suggested Barbara must be sexually starved after being away from her husband. He suggested fixing the problem right then. Barbara felt trapped.

Just then a customer returned. He had forgotten his gloves in the convention area. He found the gloves on a chair near Barbara's exhibit and stuffed them in his pocket. Barbara rushed to him and pleaded, "Please, may I walk out with you?" She walked past her taunters and out the convention center. She hailed a taxi, rode to her hotel, ran to her room and locked the door. There she waited for five hours until flight time. She was severely shaken. She never left her room while waiting for her flight. What Barbara thought was a warm and friendly situation turned threatening.

Barbara related this true story one afternoon over lunch. When someone asked her, "How do you plan to insure your safety in the future?" She replied, "I'll make sure a male crew member is with me at all times!" I questioned, "Can you guarantee a man will always be there to protect you?" She shrugged her shoulders. "You could learn prevention skills to keep yourself from becoming a victim," I suggested. "Oh no," she said, "I could never do that!"

Barbara has accepted her freedom but she chooses not to accept the responsibility for her own safety. In the next situation a young woman is inexperienced. She is just beginning to appreciate some freedom when the responsibilities come bearing down.

It was almost 6 o'clock. Cheerleading practice had taken longer then usual. Susan was a junior varsity cheerleader. The Tigers were playing their first game of the season, so the Tigerettes were practicing late. Susan was tired and sweaty. She stepped out of the gymnasium into the warm evening air with the other cheerleaders. "Oh," she said, "I forgot my math book. I've got an exam tomorrow first period. If I don't study I'll flunk for sure."

"See you tomorrow Susan," called several girls as Susan walked back to her locker. She opened her locker and took out her math book. When she reached the parking lot Mrs. Green, the cheerleading sponser, and the other cheerleaders were gone. A breeze tugged her long hair as she walked. Suddenly a whistle cut the air. It came from behind the right wing of the school. Several high school boys hung out there when they wanted to smoke. Then she heard a voice say, "Lookee at her. Ain't that little miss stuck up herself? Now she's a cheerleader she doesn't have time for anybody else."

"Yeh," came another voice, "we really should show her a thing or two." Susan's heart beat rapidly in her chest. She didn't know what to do. Nothing in school, nothing her parents said had prepared her for this scene.

Susan did not escape from this experience unscathed. She was molested, not raped. Yet the experience so effected her, her family sought counseling for her. A year later Susan entered Martial Arts training in an attempt to build her confidence.

They were in southern Minnesota. Rachael and Joyce had spent the entire day training bankers to manage their time effectively.

They started out the training session at 7:45 am. When they finished it was 6 o'clock and they were tired and hungry.

"I'd sure like a pizza and a beer," said Rachael, "my throat's dry and my feet hurt. There's supposed to be a good spot to eat deep dish pizza on 2nd Avenue. Let's eat before we head out." Joyce agreed as she was hungry also.

As they walked into the restaurant the sun sat low on the horizon. The restaurant was empty. After several pieces of pizza, beer for Rachael and coffee for Joyce, they were starting to feel full. While they ate the sun set, and the restaurant suddenly brimmed with activity. They paid their bill, got their coats and started toward the door. They still had 200 miles of road to cover before their day was done. Rachael was chattering about the workshop success as she walked ahead out the restaurant door. Joyce followed her outside and immediately sensed movement in the parking lot. Without pausing, Rachael continued to talk as she walked toward the car.

"Rachael," Joyce cautioned as she put her hand on Rachael's sleeve, "wait!" Rachael stopped and looked questioningly at Joyce and asked, "What's wrong?"

"Something doesn't feel right," she responded. "Walk back toward the restaurant with me."

"Why?" Rachael asked. "We want to get going. We've still got four hours of driving."

"Rachael," Joyce hissed, "shut up and come with me, now!" Rachael looked shocked. Joyce had never used that tone of voice before. Rachael shrugged her shoulders and followed Joyce back inside the restaurant.

What Joyce noticed when she stepped outside, was three men standing next to her car. They were leaning against the car next to her's. They could have been just talking, or they could have been waiting for a victim.

Joyce stood at the door and watched. The three didn't move. By this time Rachael saw who she was observing.

"It's just three men talking!" Rachael said. "Is that why we came back?"

"Rachael," Joyce explained, "there are three men near my car. We don't know what their intentions are. Each of those men is a potential rapist, mugger or thief."

"Aw, come on," Rachael replied. "You're going a little overboard, aren't you? Isn't everyone innocent until proven guilty?"

"No," Joyce responded, "if you're ever in a situation where you might be a victim, people are guilty until proven innocent. In other words, you must view each person as a potential problem."

"But you've got Karate training," said Rachael.

"My Karate training has made me aware of dangerous situations," replied Joyce.

"But this isn't a dangerous situation," said Rachael.

"Then let me describe what's happening," Joyce said. "First we're in a strange restaurant. The restaurant is off the beaten path. Second," she said, "it is dark out. The parking lot is dimly lit, and there are three men lounging near my car. Third," she continued, "Those men are still lounging near my car. They could be waiting for a friend inside, but I don't see anyone here who's leaving. They could be waiting for someone who is coming, but if they are, why don't they come in and order something to drink while they wait. Fourth, they could be waiting for a victim."

"What are we going to do?" Rachael asked. "We can't stay here all night."

Just then a police car cruised slowly through the parking lot. As headlights flashed on the men they ducked into a car. An engine started and they drove away.

"Now we can go," Joyce said to Rachael. "Let's get to the car." Her keys were in her hand. She knew exactly where the car was parked. The police car was still in the parking lot. When they were securely locked in the car, Rachael questioned Joyce.

"What would you have done if the police hadn't come?" she asked.

"I'd have had many choices," Joyce explained. "I would have considered my options thoroughly before acting. I could have gone to the owner of the restaurant and asked if she or he knew the three men. I could have asked someone to escort me to my car. I could have asked someone to watch until I was safely in my car. Or," she continued, "I could have taken more drastic action. I could have called the police and said I was in an uncomfortable situation and asked for a patrol car. I could have asked a mixed group of people if I might walk with them to the parking lot. Or," she said, "I could have waited to see if they were waiting for a friend. I would not, however, enter a situation where I had the opportunity to become a victim. It's important to recognize we always have choices. It's our choices that determine whether or not we become victims."

Joyce accepted both the freedom and her responsibility for her safety. Rachael accepted her freedom and perhaps unknowingly she refused responsibility for her own safety. As women accept and appreciate more freedom, they need to also accept the responsibility that accompanies the freedom. Many women view the world as Rachael, unaware, or as Susan, inexperienced, or as Barbara, abdicating personal responsibility. To remain safe and continue appreciating freedom, women will have to view the world like Joyce, alert and responsible.

Often it is difficult even for the alert responsible woman to keep herself safe because of social attitudes toward women and rape. Betty met considerable odds when she attempted to use safety skills in the following story.

When the evening meeting ended it was 10:30. Because the meeting often ran late, the board members preferred to meet in a member's home rather than at corporate headquarters. The director walked to the door with his guests and said, "Good-bye."

On the steps Betty turned to one of the men and said, "My car is parked down that dark street." The director's home, a large rambling colonial, was mentioned in many articles as an historic site. The entire street was viewed by many as a walk back through history. This beautiful street was a block away from a high crime neighborhood. Betty knew this when she asked, "Is anyone walking my way?" After several board members responded "No" and explained they had parked in the opposite direction, Betty suggested, "Let's use the buddy system and check on each other. In fact, if someone will walk me to my car, I'll be happy to drive him to his car." One of the men laughed and responded, "A women's libber like you should be able to take care of herself." One of the other women laughed and retorted, "If someone tries to rape you, just lie back and enjoy it." Betty walked to her car alone.

Each person in this situation is guilty of aiding crime. Rape is a serious crime of violence. The responses to Betty's request for help are indicative of attitudes in society toward crimes against women. You've probably heard somebody say, "Well, if rape is inevitable why don't you just lie back and enjoy it?" The underlined assumption is that you can enjoy something because it is inevitable.

Can you imagine someone saying, "If you're being beaten, just lay back and enjoy it?" Or someone saying, "It's inevitable that your jewelry is going to be stolen so enjoy it?" Or, "Count out the money to the robber and enjoy it." These are the same type of statements with a different crime. It is important to remember that rape is a crime.

Understanding assault situations may help women remain safe. Three different types of situations are common in sexual assaults. The most common situation is the cliche many believe about all sexual assaults. In this situation an unknown assailant surprises a woman and rapes her. The environment can be anywhere from a supermarket parking lot to a sunny afternoon in the park. The assailant in this situation is usually the type of masculine man who works to be aggressive. He tends to fear any type of sensitivity or softness and usually lacks concern for others. To prove his aggressiveness he needs someone to be weaker. He may even be frightened by characteristics of himself that he perceives to be feminine. For whatever reasons he usually fears and hates women. This is usually the most violent type of rape. The rapist wants to degrade, humiliate and in almost every sense destroy the female he chooses.

The second situation is when the man is a "visual acquaintance." The victim is surprised or caught off guard by a man whom she has previously seen but doesn't know well. He may be the man at the flower shop or the newstand, or he may ride the same bus or shop at the same grocery store. The victim doesn't know the assailant but she has been in contact with him. This assailant watches for the opportunity to have intercourse with the woman under circumstances where she is unlikely to tell anyone. He believes sex is something he has the right to take. When he rapes a woman, he believes he's getting a "good deal" because he doesn't have to pay for the sex in any way. He likes the idea of getting something for nothing. He tends to see women as objects for him to use. He doesn't see his actions as hurtful. He's not purposely humiliating a woman. He's just getting what he wants. This type of assailant uses only the force necessary to get what he wants.

The third type of situation is the rape on a date. The victim knows the rapist and is on a date with him. He manipulates the situation until he is sure of the outcome. This rapist believes all women want sex with him. They just need to be coaxed out of their inhibitions. He comes across as charming and then when the woman is alone with him, he pleads passion and rapes her. He rationalizes that she wasn't raped, he just had to coax her a little. This type of rape maybe a common occurance, but there are no statistics. Some women may not report this rape because they are unsure whether or not they've been raped. Many women are conditioned to see rape as something that happens with a stranger. Because many people believe rape occurs only in dark alleys or in tenderloin districts, they may not believe the woman was raped if she reports it. Actually, rape can happen anywhere; on a date, in your home, in a car, etc. It is estimated that approximately one half of sexual assaults are committed in the victim's home. The situation may occur like this.

Sixteen year old Kelly will be a Junior in high school. During her summer vacation, while working at a local drug store, she met a nice young man. Tim, who is 18, recently graduated from high school. His family moved into Kelly's neighborhood a month ago. Tim joined the Air Force and will be leaving for boot camp sometime in September.

On their third date they stop for a pizza on the way home from a movie. When Tim drops Kelly off he notices that the lights are off.

"Mom went with Dad on an overnight business trip," explains Kelly. "Mom wanted to get some shopping done in Knoxville."

It doesn't occur to Kelly not to confide in Tim. She's been out with him three times. She likes him and considers him trustworthy. Kelly's parents never gave a second thought to leaving sixteen year old Kelly alone for the night. They have good close neighbors who have agreed to keep an eye on her.

Tim asks Kelly if he can come in. Kelly says, "I don't think it's a good idea. I have to get up early for work tomorrow." Tim is charming and convinces her he won't stay long.

They sit on the living room couch and talk. Kelly suggests that he leave. Tim agrees to go but asks for a good night kiss. They kiss passionately. At first Kelly enjoys the kiss but Tim doesn't stop. She begins to struggle. He throws her on the couch and rapes her. When he finishes he apologizes and pleads passion.

"You really got me going Kelly. When you started kissing me like that I couldn't help myself. It's as much your fault as it is mine. You've been teasing me all night. You wore tight pants. You held my hand. That kiss was it. I couldn't control myself anymore. It's as much your fault as it is mine."

When he leaves Kelly says nothing. She's ashamed. She can't tell her parents, that would be too embarrassing. What if her parents think she did do something wrong. She wasn't supposed to let anyone in the house after all. Kelly is not only the victim of rape, but she feels somehow it was her fault she was raped. In fact Kelly may not be sure she's been raped. Kelly like many women may believe that rape can't happen on a date.

The three sexual assault situations are so common, many people question whether the present rape statistics are an accurate representation of the total number of rapes. Some even suggest that present statistics are only a fraction of the actual rapes which occur. This doesn't take into account other rape situations such as incest rape, or spouse rape, which are not discussed here. Many women realize they are victims of rape when they see the definition: rape is being forced to take part in or perform a sexual act against your will.

The looming question is "What can women do to remain safe from sexual assault?" A woman has many actions she can take to insure her safety:

I   Self Defense Training.

    A woman may still find herself in a situation where there is no possibility of fighting, but at least she has the option. Check your area for Marital Arts schools.

II   Practice Visualizing Dangerous Situations. Then Practice Visualizing Quick Alternatives That Would Work.

    Some situations you may want to visualize are as follows. Be sure to develop 3-5 usable alternatives. See page 56 for ideas from the alternative grid.

    A. You're standing on a street corner in your neighborhood, a car pulls up and blocks your path. What are your alternatives?

    B. You're unlocking your door and you feel "uncomfortable" about entering your house or apartment. What are your alternatives?

    C. You're leaving an evening meeting and your car is parked three blocks away. What are your alternatives?

III   Be Alert To Any Unusual Behavior.

A man appears to be watching you. People loitering for no reason. Be alert to anything that looks out of the ordinary.

IV   Be Aware of "Space and Territory" Rights.

Be aware of anyone who moves into your personal space. If you feel someone is too close, then he is. Look alert and choose your alternatives.

V   Pay Attention to Your Intuition.

If a situation doesn't feel right be cautious. If something feels wrong, react like it is wrong.

VI   Be Wary of Courtesy.

Aggressors often use a victim's code of courtesy against her. Because she is pleasant and nice she can be maneuvered into victim behaviors.

VII   Continually Know and Plan Your Alternatives.

Don't be afraid! Be alert to your environment and your choices!

VIII   Use Habits of Safety in Your Car.

    A. Always keep car doors locked, even when parked in your driveway. The only time your car should be unlocked is when you are getting in or out of it.

    B. Keep your windows rolled up. If the weather is warm, crack the window 2 or 3 inches. If someone reaches in you can roll the window up on his hand.

- C. Keep your car in good running condition.
- D. Make it a rule to fill your tank as soon as the gas gauge reads one quarter of a tank.
- E. Don't pick up strangers for any reason. If someone is stalled on the road, stop at a service station and send help back for them. Don't stop.
- F. Park your car in safe, well lighted areas.

IX Use the Buddy System.

Whenever possible walk with a friend. If both people are driving, both walk to one car then drive together to the second car. The driver of the first car stays and watches until the second driver is in the car with the door locked and the car is started.

X On Public Transportation.

If you use public transportation, stay alert to unusual situations or people. Don't sleep!

XI Walking.

When walking be cautious of hiding areas such as trees, shrubbery and corners.

XII Use Habits of Safety in Your Home (also see Chapter III)

- A. Don't allow strangers in your home without proper identification. Find out who's at your door before you open it.
- B. Keep a telephone near your bed for emergency use.
- C. Have a place to retreat in your home. Put a bolt lock on your bedroom door so that you can retreat there if someone invades your home. Then call for help.
- D. Choose to live in a safe neighborhood.
- E. Have your lights and radio on a timer so that your house looks occupied when you're gone.
- F. Lock doors even for short errands such as taking out the garbage or getting the mail.

G. Choose your home or apartment cautiously. Use the safety checklist.

　　　_____ Are there good locks on all doors and windows?
　　　_____ Is this a secure building?
　　　_____ Are there well lit streets and parking areas?
　　　_____ Are laundry and storage areas secured for safety?

In this age of new opportunity for women, there is also new responsibilities. With increased awareness and well developed safety skills, women have the opportunity to enjoy their freedom and remain safe.

9
Please, Help the Children

It's disturbing when children are victims. Many parents admit, "I don't want to think about my children in a situation where they could be hurt or molested." It is unpleasant to consider children as victims, yet awareness of the danger may prevent children from coming to harm. Children need clear concise information about how to remain safe. Adults, who refuse to give children information about nonvictim behaviors, limit a child's resources in dangerous circumstances. Children who have information about remaining safe, feel more secure and confident. Their fear doesn't immobilize them because they have alternatives of actions.

Many people ask the qustion, "Who could hurt a child?" Those who could harm a child fall into three categories:

1) other children

2) strangers

3) friends or relatives

Other children can be potential aggressors. Many people are familiar with the bully, a character that pops up frequently on playgrounds and in neighborhoods. Often there are groups of children that band together to rule the play area. Whatever the situation, because of other children, a child may feel helpless and powerless as Christopher did in the following situation.

Christopher was small for his age. All of the other boys in his class were much bigger. He was hoping he would grow fast. He was the smallest boy in the third grade. Because he was small, it seemed many of the bigger boys liked to pick on him, especially at noon recess. As long as the teacher was around he felt safe. Some teachers didn't pay attention at recess though, and then he felt scared.

After a hot lunch, consisting of macaroni and cheese with peanut butter sandwiches, it was time for noon recess. Christopher liked to stay near Mrs. Crochran. She was one of his favorite teachers. She said she liked playground duty and that being outside was good for you. He was standing near Mrs. Crochran when Shelly fell off the swing. As she landed, her hands and knees dug into the gravel under the swing. When she stood up, tears ran down her face and her mouth was wide open. Christopher figured she was screaming, but you couldn't hear the scream over the playground noise. Mrs. Crochran ran to Shelly and helped her limp into the school. Christopher was left standing alone. He stood alone quite sometime before the bell rang. As Christopher was standing next to the door he was first in line. Several boys tried to crowd in front. He said to them, "No. I was here first." One of the bigger boys pushed him hard. Christopher sat down on the sidewalk with a thud.

"You're a little baby," said the big boy, "and little babies go to the end of the line."

Christopher was afraid. He picked himself up and started toward the end of the line. As he started back another boy stuck out his foot and tripped Christopher. He fell again. He picked himself up again. His head hung, but he made it to the end of the line without crying. Then a large tear slipped down his check.

Nothing his teachers or his parents had taught him had prepared Christopher for this situation. Christopher, in third grade, was already learning what it's like to be a victim.

Certain information could help Christopher handle his situation. First he needs to learn the proper stance, which communicates "I am balanced. I will not be a victim." Then Christopher needs to learn assertive hand gestures that communicate "Stop, leave me alone."

(See Chapter 4.) Christopher also needs to practice assertive verbals such as, "Leave me alone." Last, Christopher with the help of his parents, needs the opportunity to consider his alternatives. In the following dialogue a parent helps Christopher discover his options.

> Parent: If someone pushes you out of line, what could you do?
>
> Christopher: I could tell the teacher.
>
> Parent: That's one choice, let's see how many others you can think of. What else can you do?
>
> Christopher: I can go to the end of the line and not say anything.
>
> Parent: Now you have two choices. Is there anything else you could do?
>
> Christopher: I could say "Stop pushing" and get back in line.
>
> Parent: Good! Now you have three choices, what else can we think of that you could do?

When Christopher realizes that he has many alternatives in this situation he will begin to feel more in control of himself. He may not be able to control his environment but he has power over his own actions.

Parents need to discuss alternatives with children. Even silly answers can be valuable as children will be able to laugh and put the situation in perspective. The alternative game can be a delightful way to help children consider a range of behaviors which could keep them safe.

Guidelines for the Alternative Game.

I A Situation is Described.

> Example: What would you do if someone pushed you down at recess?
>
> Example: What would you do if someone you've seen me talk to asked you to go home with them?
>
> Example: What would you do if someone you've never seen before, offered you candy?

II List **all** of the child's answers, even the wrong one, such as "I'd eat the candy a stranger offered me."

III Parents add alternatives to the list.
IV Go through the list with the child. Discuss each alternative.
Explain why you would not use some of them.
Explain which ones would be the best to use.
Explain which alternatives you use first, second, etc.

To develop more alternatives, check the alternative grid on page 56.

The alternatives may range from running to fighting. In the following story, Billy's parents wanted him to have a full range of alternatives.

His name is William but everyone calls him Billy. The blond haired cherub was 10 years old when I first met him. His parents brought him to my Karate school. As I watched Billy's first lesson from the back of the gym, his mother explained to me in low tones that Billy was frequently picked on in school. As a last resort, she brought him to Karate so he could learn self defense skills. At the same time she voiced her concern that Karate training might turn Billy into a bully. After a few weeks, I began to notice Billy in class. He seemed to grow a little bolder and more confident. His large blue eyes began to sparkle. He talked and joked when I saw him outside class.

One day after a hard workout, Billy stood in front of me at the water fountain. Out of curiosity I asked, "Billy, do you get picked on at school anymore?" He turned to me and grinned, "Naw, since I take Karate nobody picks on me."

"Have you ever been in a fight?" I asked. "Have you ever used your Karate?"

Again the slow grin, "No," Billy said. "I've never had to use it. I don't know why. Kids used to pick fights with me but when they found out I was taking Karate, they left me alone. I never had to use it. I've never wanted to use it," he said, "but I know I can. Maybe that's why they leave me alone."

Many children can benefit from physical defense training as an alternative to help them remain safe. Children can develop fine kicking techniques that will even deter the adult aggressor.

Children also need clear information about a serious problem to their safety. Parents need to inform their children about child molestation. It actually promotes confidence in children when they know what to expect and are prepared to handle it. We don't need to scare our children with all the details of molestation, but children do need simple information. Without this simple information children may not know they are victims of molestation, as was true in the following situation.

One evening after dinner, an old friend and I sat talking and sipping coffee. I don't remember how the subject came up, but this is the story he told me.

He had grown up in a small town in the heartland of America. Every Sunday afternoon the local boys were invited to use the indoor swimming pool, free of charge. It may have been a throwback to the days of skinny dipping at the old swimming hole, but the boys were allowed to swim au natural. Each Sunday afternoon, winter and summer, twenty to thirty young boys skinny dipped for an hour in the afternoon. All the boys agreed it was fun. Of course there was a chaperone. He was a young man well liked by the community. He taught in one of the local schools and counciled youth in his church.

The boys always had to take a shower before they went into the pool. It was particularly important to the chaperone that the boys were clean. He would stand in the shower doorway and check each boy for cleanliness. About every fourth or fifth boy needed to be recleaned. The chaperone would grab a bar of soap, soap up the offender's genitals and send him back into the shower. Many of the boys disliked the procedure, but they liked the swimming. No one thought of reporting this unusual behavior.

It wasn't until years later when the chaperone was caught molesting a young boy, that parents and teachers in the community put the pieces together and realized the chaperone had been a child molester for many years.

The sex crime statistics concerning children are depressing. The crimes range from molestation and indecent exposure to rape. To guard against these crimes, children need some basic prevention guidelines, in addition to the standard rule, "Don't talk to strangers."

PREVENTION Guidelines For Children

1. Always check with a parent or trusted adult before accepting anything from strangers.
2. Always check with parent or trusted adult before entering a home or riding with an adult, even if you recognize the adult.
3. Know where your parents or a trusted adult can be reached at all times.
4. Always have a "safe quarter" with you so that you can use a telephone to reach help. If no one answers at your number, dial 0 and tell the operator what wrong. Be sure to say "I need help" or "Please help me."
5. Do not let anyone rub or touch your intimate body parts. Intimate body parts are usually those covered by underwear. If someone tries to do this, tell a parent or trusted adult immediately!
6. Beware of shortcuts that take you down alleys or into unfamiliar areas.
7. Tell your parents or trusted adult about any situation or person that doesn't feel right.
8. Report to parents or trusted adult any unusual behavior like a man who watches the playground or tries to talk to children.
9. Do not give any information to callers over the phone. Never tell your name or address to a caller. Never tell a caller that you are alone.
10. Do not let anyone into your house without your parents permission.
11. If a car stops on the street and a stranger calls to you, do not go near the car, as they could grab you and pull you into the car.

Parents need to help children develop awareness not fear. One of the ways to do this is role play situations with your children. Describe the situation to the children. You play the stranger's role and let the child play himself. Some valuable situations to role play are as follows:

I   You are walking home from school. A car stops, someone rolls down the window and says, "Hey kid. Come over here. I wanna talk to you."

Correct safety response: Run the opposite direction the car is travelling, then go home immediately and tell your parent or trusted adult.

II You are in the grocery store and a stranger is watching you.

Correct safety response: Go to the nearest trusted adult or parent and tell them.

III You are at home. Your parent is gone for a brief period of time and someone knocks on the door. You are not expecting anyone.

Correct safety response: Do not open the door. Wait until your parent returns. If it is important the person will return.

IV Your parent is gone and the telephone rings.

Correct safety response: Answer the phone. Do not give your name even if asked. Instead ask, "Who are you calling?" Do not reveal you are home alone. Instead ask, "Mom is in the shower, may I have her call you back?" Or, "Dad is napping and I'm not supposed to wake him. I can tell him to call you back when he wakes up."

Many parents are afraid of frightening their children by talking about "weird or evil strangers". The purpose is not to frighten children but help them develop awareness of potentially dangerous people. It's important for children to understand; "the majority of people are helpful and kind, but there are some people who are not!" It's not always possible to tell the helpful, kind people from the others. That's why children must be cautious.

With help children can develop safety skills and prevention defense habits. Hopefully, when our children have the knowledge and skills to remain safe, there will be no victim children.

10
Should I Fight?

"If I am attacked should I fight?" is a significant question. A question every individual must consider and resolve personally for him or herself. There appear to be diametrically opposed opinions on whether or not people should fight when they are attacked. One opinion is; If you are attacked fight immediately. Another opinion is; Don't fight. You may inflame your attacker. Some experts believe fighting is the first resort. Others only fight as a last resort. Still others do not consider fighting an alternative. Whether or not you choose to fight depends on the situation and your capabilities. If you choose to fight, know something about self defense and be 100% committed to hurting or disabling your attacker.

Old movies typically portray helpless females who are molested by strong men. The female strikes the aggressor's chest with her open palms as she cries, "Don't hurt me, leave me alone." Perhaps those women thought they were fighting. They weren't. An open hand on a man's chest will rarely cause injury or deter an attacker.

If you choose to fight, know your target areas and your weapons. Target areas refer to spots on the attacker's body that are vulnerable to pain and injury. A properly made fist, an elbow, a knee, the heel of the foot, even your head can be a weapon which can cause injury or deter your attacker. Knowledge of target areas and of your own physical weapons is not enough! To effectively fight an attacker an individual needs practice and training. There's a big difference between knowledge and application. A person may have the knowledge of target areas, such as instep, shin and knees, and physical weapons such as elbows, knees or feet, but it takes practice to move the elbows, knees or feet in such a manner so as to connect with a target. Self defense or fighting is a physical activity that needs physical training. To teach someone how to ride a bicycle, you might talk about it, or explain the mechanics of a bicycle. Finally the best way to ride a bike is to get on the bike and practice. The first time someone rides a bicycle he or she may be a bit wobbley. They may need training wheels for a time. After a period of practice, the individual begins to acquire the physical ability to ride a bicycle. Once they've mastered the action of bicycle riding, they rarely forget it. Years later they can straddle a bike and recall the activity.

This is also true in physical self defense training. Once the physical defense reaction is practiced enough, it becomes a natural physical behavior. Many people have expressed the concern they will react too quickly because of defense training. It is unlikely your body will turn into a deadly weapon which reacts at the slightest noise. It is likely that you will gain the ability to use your fists, elbows and feet if you choose in a defense situation.

If you personally feel fighting is an option, then seek out martial arts or self defense training. Even a short course in self defense can train you to injure or deter an attacker. Many people feel uncomfortable the first time they try a new physical behavior. Whether water skiing, riding a bike, taking Karate, or learning to throw a pot on a potter's wheel, the first time we try the action it may feel uncomfortable. I felt uncomfortable the first time I attended a Karate class.

I changed into the stiff white uniform I'd been given for my first Karate lesson. The white cotton was starched and felt scratchy on my skin. The uniform was the traditional kimono sytle garb worn in martial arts schools. There were no zippers or buttons on the uniform, only small white strings which tied together to keep the top closed. A draw string for the waist held the trousers up. It took me several minutes to figure out how all the pieces and strings fit together.

I walked out of the dressing room into the hall feeling strange, and vaguely aware I was wearing something like my pajamas in public. There were seven other students dressed in the same white pajamas looking as uncomfortable as I felt. We stood silently waiting for someone to tell us what to do next.

A man walked out of the gym. He was dressed in a red kimono uniform. Across his back, gold lettering spelled his name. Belting the uniform was a worn and frayed black belt. He introduced himself, then asked the eight of us to form a line in the gym and bow. He explained that bowing was a sign of respect.

To begin the class we bowed to the instructor. The instructor was another man dressed in red with a black belt around his waist. He spoke quickly and enthusiastically to us about the benefits of karate. He mentioned the benefits as; self defense, exercise, weight control, discipline and a new feeling of physical confidence. Out of the corner of my eye I could see the other students standing in line. One woman and six men. I wondered if they were as nervous as I was. The instructor paused and asked if we had any questions. I had a lot of questions such as, "Do we have to fight the first day?" "Do you get hurt when you fight?" "Do you have to fight at all?" and "Is this dangerous?" I asked none of my questions. In fact no one asked any questions, so the instructor continued.

We sat on the floor and began stretching exercises that loosen the muscles. When we completed the stretching, the instructor demonstrated a back fist and a back punch. He explained target areas to aim for. Then with the safety of body shields, padded bolisters held by a partner, we were able to practice our back fists and back punches to target areas.

Before the class ended we paired off with a partner. One partner was instructed to grab the other partner tightly around the shoulders. Then the instructor demonstrated how to release the hold and escape from the attack. Each partner played both roles of attacker and defender. In the beginning we walked through the movements slowly. Then we practiced on our own. Before we left the class, we demonstrated our escape at top speed.

At each consecutive lesson we learned another self defense skill. The first time my partner really grabbed me, I felt paralyzed. After

SHOULD I FIGHT?

the tenth lesson I could respond without panicking. As I no longer panicked when I was attacked, I began to comfortably respond with my defensive actions.

Without training, many people freeze when they are attacked. An attack is usually a surprise and catches the victim totally off guard. The experience of being attacked in a safe environment, a situation where the individual will not be harmed, can help develop a context where by an individual can respond to attack situations more effectively. The Karate instructors were purposefully simulating a "safe attack", or a situation where we would not be harmed.

Often people question, "Does Karate training work? After all, you're not in a real attack situation, and don't hurt your opponent." That is true. In a Karate class you do not intentionally injure your oppponenent. You are careful of your partner's safety and health, and your partner is careful of yours. When practicing self defense behaviors. It is not necessary to injure your attacker to prove you can defend yourself. Imagine if we taught life saving by actually drowning people? That doesn't sound productive. Instead, in life saving class, a victim acts as if he is drowning. The same thing is true in martial arts classes and self defense training. An individual receives solid experiences which develop healthy responses in self defense situations.

Many books on self defense have extensive pictures describing what to do if you are attacked. Pictures can give you knowledge but they can not give you the practice you need to apply self defense in a dangerous situation. For this reason no pictures appear in this chapter. For this reason I suggest you seek a martial art's school and practice those life saving behaviors. Here are some questions to help you choose the best martial art's school or self defense course.

1) Does the school specifically teach self defense? Many martial arts schools focus on competition fighting. In competition fighting, the students learn different movements for martial arts sports. As in any sport, there is a way to score points. The focus is learning to execute certain movements usable in the ring or on the competition mat. Some of the maneuvers may be

valuable in a self defense situation, yet you do not want to spar your attacker. You want to injure your attacker and get away. Find a school that directs its energies toward self defense, so that you learn what to do when you're attacked and choose to fight. Remember, there will be no crowds or ringmaster, and no one to call foul. There will only be you fighting for your life.

2) Is student safety a priority? You may want to ask the instructors what they do to insure the safety of their students. Do they use safety pads, or protective gear? Do they take proper precautions so that neither you nor your partner will be injured?

3) How much does it cost? Is this price in line with your budget? How many courses or lessons do you get for the fee? Is the fee refundable if you decide not to continue? What does the fee include?

4) Does the school understand your priorities? You may be interested in self defense. The martial arts school may be interested in selling you a black belt course. Will the school help you meet your needs?

5) What will the self defense course teach you? You may want to ask, "What is the outcome? What will I be able to do when I finish the course? What moves are taught? What are the basic kicks or punches or moves that I will learn." Ask for their self defense lesson plan.

6) What are the rules of the school? Martial arts schools have rules that range from no chewing gum, to no loud talking. Find out what the rules are before you enroll.

7) What is the philosophy of the school? Some martial arts schools have the philosophy "fight only as a last resort." What is the school philosophy, and does it match your own.

8) When are the class hours? Are they at a good time for you?

9) What is the physical endurance ability you need to take a class? Many martial arts schools push students until they drop. Other martial arts schools believe you get your physical fitness and endurance training elsewhere, and their goal is to teach techni-

11
The Experts Talk

One cold wintry afternoon, four people sat around a conference table: Gordon Franks, 1975-1980 Super Lightweight, Full-Contact Karate Champion, Pat Worley, 1975-76 National Karate Champion, John Worley, Chairman of the Board of Commissioners for The Professional Karate Association, Larry Carnahan, World Ranked Full Contact Fighter. When polled they gave various responses to several questions about attitude, behavior, and self defense. When asked: "What type of attitude is important in a self defense situation?" they answered:

One of confidence but not superiority. An attitude that allows you to humanize yourself to the attacker, and allows you to relate to him. Remember, you must be able to remain calm and rational so that you can judge how to react to your attacker. If you are out of control, you may lose opportunities for escape and will stand no chance of gaining control of the situation yourself.

In a dangerous situation, an individual needs a confident attitude with a realistic perception of what is really happening in the situation and the environment.

A person needs to project an image of confidence. That image of confidence will be revealed especially through eye contact. Many victims have immediate gaze aversion, or they can't look the aggressor in the eyes. Your attitude in a self defense situation should project confidence as opposed to withdrawing.

Your attitude is your awareness and your awareness needs to begin before any self defense situation occurs. Each individual needs to be aware of potential situations. You need to start your defense before anything happens.

If you are in the right, you should never back off because of physical or psychological intimidation. An aggressor commonly recognizes that the other person is right, and this gives the potential victim an edge. If the potential victim reflects an attitude of confidence in his or her position, and an understanding that he or she is right, many times the aggressor will back down. Above all be confident. calm, relaxed and think.

The next question the experts answered was: "What type of behavior is necessary in a self defense situation?"

Behavior that will not antagonize your attacker, and appropriate behavior for the situation. There is no sense in yelling if there is no one to hear you. Each attack situation is different. Depending on which type of person you are dealing with, you should change the behavior you use. Think! Be intelligent. Know as much about yourself as you can. Know as much about your surroundings as you can. Assess your attacker. If the situation has the potential of deteriorating into a physical confrontation, you must be willing to totally commit yourself to doing everything possible to stop the aggressor. Any half hearted attempt will fail. Since fighting is an animalistic mode of behavior, you must be willing to become as animalistic as is necessary in order to survive.

When you are threatened physically, you must be flexible. Keep your thoughts open and watch your timing. Ask yourself, "When is the right time to run? When is the right time to fight?"

Panic is a negative thought. Remain calm, use your adrenalin to increase your thinking speed. Tell yourself I'm here and it's for real. Then ask yourself, "What can I do?" If something is going to happen, be first to act. If you're truly convinced something is going to happen, don't be afraid to take the initiative.

to become aware of people around you, and whether or not they are paying particular attention to you. Learn to observe others, especially when you are writing out a check, or giving someone your address.

It's very important to look confident. This means acting as if you know exactly where you are going what you are doing. This may mean acting like someone is waiting for you even if no one is. Awareness is really becoming more adept at defensive living.

When asked: "How do you know a real situation that needs self defense?", the experts responded:

One of the ways to tell whether or not it's a life threatening situation, is if you feel threatened. If you feel in danger, regardless of what the situation is, you should take steps to remove yourself from that situation.

It is your judgement decision and the more aware of any and all situations the better able you are to make a good decision. The properly trained person anticipates situations and has a suitable battle plan mentally mapped out.

If you are in doubt, assume it is a real situation and take steps to either back off, become assertive, attack or make another decision. Always assume it's a real situation. Make sure that you keep yourself safe rather than being polite.

The experts agreed that most everyone could benefit from Martial Arts of Self Defense training. They stressed that everyone should learn basic defensive moves. Even the beginners can master the simple self defense techniques with a bare minimum of training.

ques for survival. Are you in physical shape to handle the class?

10) What are the ages of the students? Will you be required to keep up with younger people. If you are 40 or 50 years old, will you be in a class geared toward people who are 18 and 19? Who is the class physically geared for?

11) What is the teaching philosophy? Is it an adult class taught with respect and responsibility, or a class for children that's taught with punishment and reward? Does the teacher use an independent learning approaches where the student pushes him or herself, or does the teacher use competition where members of the class regardless of age, are pitted against each other to see who can be first, fastest, or hardest.

The responses you get to these questions will guide you toward the martial art's school or self defense class best suited for you.

If you choose to fight, it is a personal choice that depends on the situation and your abilities. If you choose to fight, you must be 100 percent committed to injuring or in someway hurting your opponent. If you choose to fight, it's unlikely you will have any other alternative available to you. It's almost impossible after trying to injure your attacker to say, "I was only joking, let's talk about it. Let's compromise." If you choose to fight, there's no turning back. You must be committed. It is important to remember that the defender or potential victim doesn't need to "win" the fight. This is no contest. The object is to cause the assailant to reconsider whether the attack is "worth it". If the assailant has a concern about his safety, he may reconsider the assault. Most assailants do not desire confrontation and will look for an easier victim. Regardless of your size, age, or sex, with training and practice you can develop skills that will injure or deter an opponent long enough for you to get away.

Epilogue

If you choose to swim alone, it doesn't mean you want to drown. If you choose to walk alone, it doesn't mean you want to be a victim. If you have been a victim, it doesn't mean you walked or talked "wrong". It's time we stopped blaming victims. Everyone should have the right to live a life safe from harm. Until our society condemns violence and crime, individuals need to be alerted to their own safety.

Martial Arts' training is suggested throughout this book, not because I want individuals fighting on every street corner, but because physical training gives the confidence to choose other alternatives.

By reading this book, you've been exposed to many alternatives. It is my wish that these alternatives will help keep you safe and alive.

Recommended Reading

Dobson, Terry & Miller Victor, **Giving In to Get Your Way**, New York, Delacorte Press, 1978

Medea, Andra, & Thompson, Kathleen, **Against Rape**, Doubleday & Doubleday Canada Ltd., Toronto, 1974

Peterson, Susan G., **Self-Defense For Women The West Point Way**, New York, Simon & Schuster 1979

Tegner, Bruce & McGrath, Alice, **Self-Defense & Assault Prevention for Girls & Women**, Thor Publishing Co., 1977,
Self-Defense for Your Child, California, Thor Publishing Co., 1976

Superintendent of Documents, **Uniform Crime Report: Crime in the United States**, U.S. Government Printing Office, Washington D.C., August, 1982

TAKING CHARGE OF YOUR OWN SAFETY

SAFE IN THE STREETS uses a direct, practical approach based on real-life stories of people who successfully prevented or stopped attacks to illustrate the range of behaviors possible in any given situation, and to reinforce the message, "You can take charge of your own life and safety."

Ms. Merwin explains how alertness, preparedness, self-confidence, and self-defense are the tools anyone can use to prevent violent crime from happening to them. SAFE IN THE STREETS explains victim behavior (the nonverbal cues and behavior which criminals use to identify easy victims), and explodes the myths which convince people that they cannot—or need not—be responsible for their own safety. Chapters also focus on appropriate self-defense behaviors for women and children.

$5.95 plus $1 postage & handling
(formerly titled: NOT A VICTIM)

Sandra J. Merwin is the founder and head of Sandra Merwin Enterprises in Minneapolis, a firm which offers training and motivational programs for corporate management teams across the nation. She is the author of a variety of learning materials and business articles. In the course of her research on this book, she earned her brown belt in karate.

THE BOOK PEDDLERS 18326 Minnetonka Blvd Deephaven, MN 55391

ORDER FORM

Please send me _____ **copies of SAFE IN THE STREETS @ $6.95 ppd. (Quantity discounts available on request.)**

☐ Check or money order enclosed payable to The Book Peddlers.
☐ Charge to _____ Visa; _____ Masterchage; exp. date _____
Acct # _____ Signature x _____

SEND TO:

NAME _____

ADDRESS _____

CITY/STATE _____ ZIP _____

PHONE _____

THE
BOOK
PEDDLERS
18326 MINNETONKA BOULEVARD
DEEPHAVEN, MINNESOTA 55391
(612) 475-3527

HV 7431 .M47 1985

89-0619

Merwin, Sandra J.

Safe in the streets

DATE DUE
FEB. 7 94

DATE DUE
APR-14-94

DATE DUE
A-03-95

ASHEVILLE-BUNCOMBE
TECHNICAL COMMUNITY COLLEGE
LEARNING RESOURCES CENTER
340 VICTORIA ROAD
ASHEVILLE, NC 28801